Ang

by Angela R. Zurita

DORRANCE PUBLISHING CO
EST. 1920
PITTSBURGH, PENNSYLVANIA 15238

Dorrance Publishing Co
585 Alpha Drive
Suite 103
Pittsburgh, PA 15238
Visit our website at *www.dorrancebookstore.com*

ISBN: 979-8-8852-7276-6
eISBN: 979-8-8852-7714-3

Prologue

I wasn't always this way, you know? I wasn't always inse- cure and stand-offish.

I didn't always come off as a hard-ass, and I used to let people walk all over me, because my family, and society said that I should. I wasn't always so distrusting of everyone, and I didn't have the idea where I believed that not everyone deserves the benefit of the doubt. I used to value the opinion of those around me, and I wasn't always willing to confront those that disrespected me. No, I used to be softer. At one point, I hoped and prayed that my family would treat me more like I belonged. I grew out of that when I realized blood is not always thicker than water. Let me share parts of my life with you, and the events that have molded me into the flawed woman that I am today—with just a little more confidence than I had before.

My name is Angela, but my therapist calls me Ang. You, my friend, can call me whatever you like. I think the best part about being open and transparent is that there's no guess work in terms of getting to know someone; no secrets. Let's get to know each other. I have been told in the past that I'm too forward, or that I'm too harsh. If you knew me years ago when I was younger, my past would show that I haven't changed very much. Actually, I believe I'm more docile as I'm coming up on my 30th birthday, but for all the wrong reasons.

Between you and me, I'm probably not the best one to attempt a book writing. My memory is terrible, and I know I've pushed so many things out, that I've literally reduced my memory to very few life events. I can't really attach certain details, like my age at certain points, only because I don't want to feel like I'm lying to you. Just know that I'm working my way from the beginning, up until becoming an adult. Just know that I appreciate you for being here, and the patience you're bound to need to have for my off the wall writing.

I want to just blurt out every bad decision, every indiscretion, to you; I want to just plainly tell you my reasoning for writing this, but that would do no justice. I don't know where you come from, or who you are; I don't know the color of your skin, your sex, your sexual orientation, or your political beliefs; I don't know if you've sinned, or if you even believe in any higher power.

What I do know is that I believe on the inside, we're all the same. I know that people experience many different things in their life from emotional highs to the deepest lows you can imagine. As human beings, I think we have more in common than some may believe. I think no amount of money, lifestyle, or status can protect us from the inevitability that at some point, some sort of negative event will change our lives forever.

In a nutshell, I am insecure, a hothead, nosy, I can be selfish at times, and, of course, jealous. Those are just the qualities I have realized and accepted about myself, and that took me a long time of many trials, and errors. In addition to those strong qualities, I am also giving, loyal, thoughtful, smart, and independent. If you do right by me, I will always do right by you. My story has been a little dark, and in the process of me sharing my story with you, I hope that I shine a little light on your story.

Chapter 1

Let's start from the beginning. I was born in Dallas, Texas. My family is fairly large, and I knew my parents to be the two people that have raised me. At times, this family unit didn't make sense to me. Pieces were missing. I have two half-brothers and two half-sisters. All of them are significantly older than myself, and each of them have their own family. I wouldn't say that I'm exactly a good fit in my family. Honestly, I would consider myself a black sheep. Growing up, I was the youngest. The baby. My parents were much older and were everyone else's grandparents, which left me as the youngest aunt to everyone. So, I had a good start, I'd say.

Let me try to paint the picture of my childhood as I remember it. My father was a hardworking man. Being a self-taught mechanic from a young age, I remember my father being able to work on pretty much anything. I thought it was absolute magic. Every morning he would wake up, pull a little black comb out of his back pocket, and slick back his hair. He would always wear the same thing, which was a pair of faded out

Dickie's, and a white t-shirt. When I was a baby, he worked for companies, but as I got older, and he got older, he started to work from home to be around for me more. He would work on customer's cars from home, and while I'm sure the neighbors didn't appreciate the noise, he had a following of customers that sought him out, because he was the only honest mechanic they knew. I've learned through the years that word of mouth is the best way to get customers to your business, and word of mouth is what my father had. The only thing my father didn't work on was airplanes, but I suppose that's because they have such strict educational requirements, and really, no one wants a plane to fall out of the sky. Go figure.

The other thing that I remember about my father, and is a fond memory, is that my father had a rocking chair in his room. He would always sit there when watching television, reading his automotive manuals when trying to figure out a problem car, but most importantly, he sat in that chair when he talked to me, or any of his grandkids, giving us advice on life. I could sit there for hours listening to this man, and honestly, if you accumulated all the time we sat there listening, it would add up to years. I learned how to do lawn work because of this man. I learned to date everything I wrote on; I learned to snap a photo any chance I got; I learned to care for the things that are yours to make them last; I learned how to be honest, and I learned how to save a penny.

My mother was a homemaker. I remember that she would stay up late after everyone had already gone to bed, and that would be her cleaning time. She would sweep, and mop, wipe down everything, and so I awoke to a pristine kitchen pretty much every morning. My parents were old fashioned, so my dad worked, and my mother would tend the house, raise me, and more often would also raise their grandkids. There was hardly ever a time that I was home with just my mother. For future reference in my writing, I'll introduce my nephew, Eric, and my niece, Vicky. Being more than eight years older than me, I remember specifically in my childhood that they were around the most.

As a young child, the two of them would let me "beat them up." I would throw blocks at Eric's head, or get piggyback rides. Vicky was always so enthusiastic with how she spoke. We would color, and even though mine was typical of a child—being outside the lines—she would praise my efforts like they belonged in a museum. I always appreciated the two of them for the role they played in my life growing up. I even remember when they would let me stay up with them, and watch *South Park*, because it was absolutely forbidden any other time. More than anything, they were the two that I had a good standing relationship with. They protected me, and molded me, even though I was a daddy's girl, and if anyone made me cry, I ran straight to him. It's funny now, because I'm sure I rubbed them both, and my mother, the wrong way with my insistence on telling my father everything under the sun.

We grew up in a quiet neighborhood. My parents bought the house back in the 80's, and never moved. Overall, it was a good environment to grow up in. Three bedrooms, one bathroom, and a small building in the backyard. Everyone in the neighborhood was friendly, but everyone stayed in their own business. That was my favorite part. I remember my father made a deal with the neighbor across the street who happened to be an artist. He made the deal that he would fix the neighbor's truck, if he painted my room with cartoon characters. So, my room became pink with Bugs Bunny, Daffy Duck, The Powerpuff Girls, Tweety Bird and others. Eventually when I got older, I had it painted over, because the Powerpuff Girls began to give me nightmares.

Yes, my childhood was memorable. When I was in the single-digit age range, I had a dog given to me. He was a chihuahua mix, all black, white feet, and a little white tip on his tail. His name was Peewee, and since the time I had him, he was the love of my life. That dog was a first, not only for me, but for my mother, because she greatly disliked the idea of having dogs. It was too late, though. That dog was mine. He watched cartoons with me, he snuggled with me, he was everywhere I was. He was the first best friend that I had.

I spent a good portion of my childhood just being a kid. I "helped" my father wash his classic Chevy truck when he parked it in the front yard. They would buy me baby pools, and set them underneath trees for shade. If there were no shade, my father would sit poolside with an umbrella for hours, so that I wouldn't burn. I remember family being over a lot for barbeques, or just to visit with my parents while I stayed around the other kids. It's easy to assume that I had a close-knit rela-tionship with my family. That assumption was wrong. I wish the positive memories were enough not to taint the rest of it. Having a good childhood, my friends, just wasn't enough.

Chapter 2

Unfortunately, the older I got, the more problems I had. I had issues with not only my relationships, but with myself. These issues didn't have a label for me back then. Growing up in an old school, Mexican-originated household, anything other than being physically sick didn't exist. So, that's where one issue existed, and I'll get into more depth as we go. Another issue was that I began to pull away from the relationships that weren't healthy for me, and again, in some eyes, this is frowned upon. Speaking for myself, when you grow up, you're generally taught that family is family. You're not allowed to sever those relationships, because they're family, "blood is thicker than water," and whatever other reasons people give to put up with toxic relationships.

I don't agree. I believe that if people consistently show you who they are, you're supposed to listen. I don't think family is necessarily who you're born with or to. Quite the contrary, I think family is made up of people that accept you for who you are; I think family is made up of people that support you in anything you strive to do, and to belittle you in ways that show the opposite does not in my mind represent family. I grew up having sleepovers at my friend's house. They weren't perfect by any means, but they had the ability to have healthy relationships with multiple people in their families. Mine was not that way. I know. I haven't a clue what went on behind closed doors. I know.

I grew up with my mother wanting me to attend church, even though she never did. She wanted me to attend with my brother, and his family. Being young, it wasn't so bad, but I couldn't help, but notice some inconsistencies, and that made me uncomfortable. I consider myself a spiritual person, but you won't find me in church every Sunday, or with the Holy Bible in my bedside table. Many wouldn't consider me a very good Christian, but I know myself well enough to know that I always try to be on the right side of things despite the consequences that await me.

I despise lying, I hate cheating, I don't condone beating around the bush, and I will never agree with something if the origin of it is greed. I can't agree with those that portray themselves as being "Holier than thou," but practices the same poor behavior that they claim to be against. Now, let me cover myself here. I am not perfect by any stretch of the imagination. I have screwed up more times than I can count, and many of those mistakes, I am still paying for. If you take nothing else from this book, take away that no matter what you've done, or what poor decision you've made, you can make something out of nothing. I know it's not easy, and whatever progress you have made so far, I'm proud of you if no one else is.

My brother is a self-proclaimed, "Man of God." For many years, I heard my mother brag about her son, the preacher, and I saw my father roll his eyes every time. My father was usually a pretty good judge of character, so when he took issue with someone, I paid attention. My brother is much older than myself, and more times than I can count, he always needed something from my parents. Tools, lawn equipment from my father, and money from my mother. In his marriage, he was the almighty, and the rest of his family needed to know. I never was behind those closed doors, but my memory has always served the faint memories of abuse from the children. Therapy now tells me that I've completely booted certain memories from my mind for the sake of my own well-being, so I will say that slaps, and the belt comes to mind. I believe that their household was run more as a bootcamp being that he was previously in the Marine Corps, but I also recall that he was dishonorably discharged, because he wasn't going to have anyone tell him what to do. This was not a "Man of God" that I would seek guidance from. Not in the least.

Needless to say, church was a no-go. As soon as I could, I stopped going, and my mother was not supportive of that choice. Luckily, I got permission from my father, and when he said I didn't have to go, that was it. So, my mother, and my brother were very much alike, and I don't say that as a compliment. This person was one of five children including myself. I don't like diving into this subject very much—hence my reluctance to tell you exactly who this person was, but hey, I trust you. Transparency, right?

Again, this is her oldest son, and if you pay attention, they were thick as thieves. This is from the eyes of a younger self. Since he spent the most time in the church, she saw him as a great success. I suppose in his own right, he was. That's just if you didn't know him very well. I remember him as belligerent, self-righteous, arrogant, loud-mouthed, and his nose so high in the air that if he stood outside in the rain, he would drown. This was the man that was either blind to, or secretly enabled, his wife's pain pill addiction. From an ex-convict, to a man of God, he would be a good example of a "rags to riches" story. Just minus the riches. If this were any other man, I would applaud the diligence of wanting to do something different. It wasn't another man, it was this man, and this man's narcissism I will always be willing to bet is what drove him to become what he did in the church. I'm not sure if he's a false prophet, or he's just really good at paraphrasing from the Bible to make other people swoon, and awe over him.

This is important to know, because this plays into the greater scheme of things. We had somewhat of a relationship when I was young. This was only because my mom would tell me to, and she would defend the venom he spewed out of his mouth, and cover it as humor that I apparently didn't have. I would cry, become frustrated, and my mother would pat him on the back, and stare at him as if he were God himself. She was almost... blind. I believe she wanted so badly for everyone in the family to fit together so badly, especially with him, that she would turn a blind eye to the mayhem if she had a chance.

He was the opposite of what I believe a good Christian is supposed to be. I don't believe you should have to shame and belittle others, because they don't fit in your small box of Christian criteria. I believe in pots calling the kettle black, and I believe a person turning their nose to other people in a way of asserting your superiority is crap. We're all born the same way, and while we may succumb to death in different ways, we're all going to be the same set of bones. For the bigger percentage of down-to-earth, good-hearted people, please keep doing what you're doing. For the smaller percentage of bad apples, I think that to be a good Christian, the church should require a heaping amount of humility to be carried by everyone instead of this superiority complex. Put your pants on the same way I do, and live your life to make it better, not more ignorant.

Chapter 3

One thing I noticed growing up was that I didn't fit in the way everyone else fit together. My other nieces and nephews all had this already-grown bond that they didn't really have to work at. When it came to myself—sure they were nice. Sure, I was loved. I was literally the baby of the family, and everyone wanted to help with the baby, but something never sat right with me. I grew up with Eric, Vicky, and my other niece, Ashley, but getting older, it just seemed a lot harder to find my place with everyone else. Not only that, but I remember hearing the phrase, *"My mom..."* I heard this phrase a lot from my older siblings growing up, and I never could put my finger on why that bothered me so much, but it did. When it was said, it carried intent.

I always thought it was, because I was disliked. Hell, that could still be the case. I'm honestly not sure. My mother's other kids were indeed her kids. My father was their step-father, and so they always called him by his first name. I don't know the details of everyone's past, and so I will try to stay within the realm of what I know for myself. As far as I know, none of them ever had an extremely close relationship with my father. I know that my two sisters had their own dad that they stayed in contact with, but I can't say I know about the father of my two brothers. So, I have four half-siblings. Stay with me here.

My mother became pregnant at a young age with one of my half-brothers. She has told me on multiple occasions that she didn't have a clue what to do as a young mom, and that times were much different back then. I know she has told me that she had broken family relationships, she was abused, and so she didn't have much support from anyone. She also said that she made many mistakes in terms of discipline, and the general raising of her kids. I feel for my mother, because the woman I know now is greatly different from the woman she describes from her past. Somewhere down the road she met my father, and when they got more serious, they moved hours away from the nonsense, and made a home there in the suburban home I've come to love, and where my roots began.

The memories I have from my childhood, they play in my head like an old home movie. It's not detailed, but I do have general memories that I've kept over the years. I remember the tiny, artificial Christmas tree that my parents got me, because I had childhood asthma, so we never had a real one. This tree stood maybe a foot and a half tall. It sat on a small table with a cover on it, and there would be a few presents sitting there waiting to be opened. Even then it wasn't the quantity, but more of the quality.

My father always had a large video camera in his hands. You know, the ones that held VHS tapes that were recorded on. He wanted to capture everything on film, and it drove my mother nuts, because she didn't want to be filmed, but we weren't going to get those moments back. So, he would sit the camera up on the tripod, and when the presents were ready, they would bring tiny me out of the bedroom in my footie pajamas, and my hair a mess. My father would try to entice me to open my own presents, but he would end up opening them up for me anyways. They would be something from the show, *Barney*. Do you remember who that is, or am I already beyond my time?

These home movies were everything to me, and my parents. I loved those memories, and being able to look back at them. While they were all different, the one common denominator that they shared was a love they had for me. My parents cherished everything that I did, and I know that they always wanted the best for me. I tell you all of this, because my mother used to tell me that she raised me differently. She said that she was much more tolerant, and soft, when she raised me.

Not everything was rainbows, and unicorns. Don't get me wrong on that note. While I don't necessarily have anything bad to say about my parents, I will say that there were certain aspects that I would've changed if I could. My parents loved me unconditionally, but I don't believe they would say the same about each other if I asked them. As far as I could remember, they never slept in the same room. I don't think I ever saw them hold hands, or compliment each other. My father financially took care of her, and me, and if she wanted something like a car, he would get it for her. My mother would cook, clean, and purchase things for him like new wallets, lawn care machines, and new tools for his work.

Sure, it seems pretty simple, but they would also call each other names, yell at one another, slam doors, etc. In a smaller home, it's hard to ignore. I heard every foul thing they ever said to each other, and I remember wondering to myself, "Why stay with each other if you don't love each other?" Even being young, it doesn't take a rocket scientist to know that people that love each other don't treat each other like they're disposable. Of course, my parents did what so many couples do: They stayed for the kids.

I respect people that try their damnedest to make marriages or relationships work so that their child(ren) have both parents. From the way I grew up, if you were to ask me as a kid, I would've told you that I would've rather had my parents split, than watch their relationship deteriorate over the years. I would've rather have been from a broken home than lived in one. Of course, that's not everyone's cup of tea, and in no way to speak for everyone. All I know is that growing up, I never learned what a healthy, appropriate relationship was supposed to look like, and that has served me poorly as an adult.

My parents were great when they were apart. Each one had their own way of how they wanted me to be raised, and that wasn't always the same. On the flip side, I learned from my father how he took care of his family. Even being old school, I understood that my father set the bar high in my mind on how a man was supposed to treat someone. Not necessarily by the way my parents got along, but how he treated me as his daughter. Otherwise, watching everyone else in my family, I don't think I ever saw anyone in my family in a healthy relationship. I know that some of them were victims of abuse, some of them were the abusers, some of them were just plainly toxic, and others just didn't have a clue.

As I grew up, something always bothered me about my family unit. My parents weren't like everyone else's parents when I was starting in elementary school. They tried their best, you know? It was just something that never made sense to me. Teachers would ask me if my grandparents were picking me up, and when I would correct them, they looked like deer in the headlights. My mother couldn't do activities like other parents, and my father tried hard, but I do remember getting games, gaming consoles, and puzzles to keep me occupied.

We had tons of baby photos of myself, videos, little trinkets that my mother kept over the years. There were certain things missing, though. I never saw photos from the hospital that would have my mother in the hospital; I never saw my original birth certificate, and my mother would tell me that when I was a newborn, that I was sickly, but she never told me how. So, all together these things always made me question what the big secret was. I tucked these questions away, because really, they weren't that important for me to answer at that time.

Chapter 4

I wasn't familiar with tragedy until I was about six years old. I had an uncle that everyone in the family called "Peewee," which was accurate, because of his much smaller stature. Per my mother, he was why we named the dog Peewee, because he, too, was small. He was naturally thin, with gray, slicked back hair, and a white beard. He carried around and played a guitar, and even though he always had a home to come to, he always preferred to be out on the streets, and panhandle with his buddies. If no one knew where he was, he was more than likely drinking underneath a bridge somewhere.

I loved my uncle. Despite his outward flaws, he was a kind, and giving man. He gave me a giant teddy bear when I was little, and later down the road he gave me another chihuahua puppy that I named Candy. One of the nights he came back from panhandling, he had me come to the coffee table in the living room, and he dumped out a white bucket of what he had collected. He pulled out this nice, blue, marble from his pile, and handed it to me. If my memory serves me correctly, it had a small dent in it, and I never mistook it for another marble. I must have held onto that particular marble for years.

Anyways, there was one night in particular that my life jumpstarted what I knew to be the real world. There's many pieces missing, but the important details are still intact. If you ever watch those movies where something bad is about to happen, and it's raining really hard outside, you'll piece together the story I'm telling. I remember that on that night, someone came, and knocked on the door during evening hours. It was already dark out, and especially with the bad weather, my parents weren't expecting anyone to come knocking.

One of my parents opened the inner wooden door, and when they were to open the outer glass door, a tall, dark figure was standing on the porch. He had a trench coat on, and if you think it sounds like a tale, I wouldn't blame you. The man asked my mom if she knew this man he was trying to identify. "That's my brother," she said. He came inside, and little me was there playing with my toys. He went on to tell her and my father that he had been killed earlier that night. They found him on a busy road after he had been part of a hit and run, then dragged down the road by another car. He was intoxicated.

I remember a really heavy silence falling over the room. I guess my best idea at that point was to try to comfort them by serving my little plastic foods. I didn't know what death was back then. I didn't know that they were talking about my uncle, and that those words would mean that he was never coming back. That was it.

Jump forward to my next memory which was at his burial. I mentally excluded everything in between. He had a viewing, and I don't remember any of that. I know that my mother said that they had a viewing for him, but in actuality, there wasn't enough of him to actually view. The casket was empty. At the burial, my memory of it is honestly a fog. I remember family being there, but everyone that stood around me, in my mind, doesn't have a face. There are no specifics. I just remember figures in black, crying, and moaning at the loss.

After that, and finally coming to the understanding about what death was, I think the only way to describe me after the fact was scared. I knew that my parents were older, and I, also, knew that if anything were to happen to one, or both of them, I would never be the same. So, I would lie in bed at night playing the worst-case scenarios, and it would keep me up for hours. I thought that was my own self-diagnosis: Fear. I thought it was an accurate reason for why I was having a difficult time.

Chapter 5

In my family, bluntness and callousness run in our blood. Everyone is so opinionated, loud, and abrasive. I'm surprised anyone finds people in our family attractive in terms of personality. In my family, it was understandable to be this way as an adult. If you portrayed these qualities as a young one, it was a sure-fire way to get into trouble. You know, the "respect your elders" rule. I didn't get spanked as a child, but I did get the heavy talks that would make me feel a million times more guilty. Everyone else got the sandal, or slipper. We would just call it, "La Chancla," or "The Flip-Flop."

Since I didn't get the corporal punishment, when I was little, anytime I witnessed something so far into left field, I had a hard time letting go. There was a day that I sat on the floor in my room with one of my nieces, playing Legos. She and I are within a year of each other, so we got along well. I remember that her mom came to pick her up one of my half-sisters. I couldn't tell you what the circumstances were leading up to that moment, but I remember she rushed into that room, and when my niece didn't hop up fast enough to leave, my half-sister slapped her across the face. Hard.

I was shocked. I stared at my niece, and her eyes welled up, but she didn't outwardly cry. They left me alone on the floor of my room, and I probably sat there for minutes before I started crying on my own. It didn't happen to me, but I felt like it may as well have. I wanted to yell at my "sister" for that and ask her what gave her the right to hit her that way. I wanted to know what she did that was so bad that she deserved her mother laying into her the way she did.

I'm a high-strung empath. Boy, if I had a quarter for every time I cried over someone else's business, I would be a very, very rich woman. I don't know about other empaths, but I cry over things that other people would probably shake their head at. I cry, and get a heavy feeling in my gut when I hear victims of abuse. I feel it in my bones when people try to go above and beyond as human beings with good deeds, donations, volunteer work... I feel big emotions when I read or see the news about victims of Hurricane Katrina, Maria, etc., or those that live in poverty that have to overcome dire circumstances to remotely reach the level of comfort in life that many take for granted. I cry at Pixar movies at the happiest of moments. I wear my emotions on my sleeve. Overall, more than likely, if you're close enough in proximity to me, if you're hurting, I will hurt with you.

Chapter 6

When I got into my double-digit ages, I had an extremely hard time managing my emotions. I had an even harder time expressing my emotions without getting frustrated, or angry. If it would get to a boiling point, I would have to walk away to my room, because I knew I wasn't going to be able to get my point across without pissing someone else off. I had a terrible time sleeping. I had a hell of a time falling asleep, and even harder time staying asleep. I would often get scolded for still being up late at night.

I wouldn't get scolded by just my parents about my forming personality habits. I would also hear all about how rude of a kid I was. I learned that I was spoiled, rude, and disrespectful. This was all from family members that didn't live in the same house as myself. That was an easy way to determine who I could, and could not talk to. What I couldn't explain to anyone at the time was the feeling of impulsiveness, even when I knew the decisions weren't in my best interest. I couldn't explain how I would feel when I tried to sleep, or the millions of ways I would feel irritable. Every noise I would hear was like nails on a chalkboard. Little noises, repetitive noises, would light my extremely short fuse, and it would make it very difficult to have a conversation with anyone.

I would lie in bed at night, and the ceiling fan would click; the other fan that I had would crackle. I could hear the tiniest sounds coming from outside the window, or the other bedrooms, and it would drive me up the wall. I had to sleep in very specific ways, because if I didn't, I would feel constricted, constrained, suffocated, and those feelings would turn into immense anxiety and frustration. Even me just rummaging through those memories to explain to you makes me feel uneasy.

These feelings eventually bled into school. Even though I did fairly well in school, my problems leaned heavily on me. For the most part I got good grades, I didn't have perfect attendance, but I was there. All the way through middle school I wasn't what I would call, "Popular." I was instead the girl that was acquainted with everyone. I can count on one hand the number of people that disliked me, and I think that's a pretty good statistic. The friends that I did have were good people, and it made a sustainable distraction from my home life.

Any school function that I had, my parents were there. There was never a question of if they would be there, or not, and I appreciated that more than anything. I was never the kid that looked into the audience, and saw two empty seats where my parents were supposed to be. What was missing more times that I noticed was that everyone else had extended family there, but I didn't. That was okay. At least, that's what I would tell myself.

Chapter 7

ears later, besides my daily dose of social interaction, I hated school. I hated to sit in classes I didn't really need, but I think that's the thought process of every kid. I already had it in my head that I wanted to be a working adult at the young age I was at. I just wanted to be independent, productive, and not have to ask anyone for money. On top of not being able to sleep at night, and dragging myself through school, I hated a good part of my life.

Around this time as a teenager, this is when I started to put a few things together. One of my half-sisters always let me come stay the night at her house. My mom would approve, but my dad was always very reluctant. This meant when they would go on vacations, and if I were invited, it was very seldom that I went. This would frustrate me greatly, because I wanted to go. I wanted to be included, but I would be at home left to entertain myself.

My nephew, Eric, had moved in with us at multiple points in his life. Whenever he was there, I was happy, because I had someone to talk to, and play games with. He acted like a big kid, except that he could drive, and that was a win-win for me. He would make me laugh at the stupid things that he would say, and even more made my mother absolutely despise taking us both to the store with her when she would have to go grocery shopping. If I went alone, it was boring, because my mother would have to go through every single aisle, and she would walk them slowly. So, when both Eric and I would go, our shenanigans would embarrass her so much that she would quickly walk away with her basket, acting like she didn't know who we were, but Eric would be in tow yelling, "Grandma! Where are you going?! You're my ride!"

"Get away from me! You're both so embarrassing!" She would yell back, and I'm laughing so hard in the clothing section, because I would hide in the clothes rack scaring people as they would walk by. I knew my mom was going to be a million times angrier if she couldn't find me. She never found me.

There were times that Eric would put his Xbox in the living room, and we would play *Call of Duty: Zombies*. I would laugh hearing him trash talk kids over the microphone, but I would laugh even harder, because my dad would often close his door so that he wouldn't have to hear us. Sometimes curse words would slip, and when that would happen, we would look at each other, and then to his door to see if he would come out to yell at us for our language. The strange thing was that when we would use actual curse words, he wouldn't come out, but as soon as Eric said, "darn," "dang" "dag-nabbot," and "sheet," he would barge out of his room telling Eric to not talk like that with me there. When I tell you how funny this was, words couldn't even begin to describe how much.

Some of my happier times were him living with us. He wasn't my nephew, he was more like my big brother, and that's what I would call him. He protected me, mentored me, and was my light in many dark times. He would often tell me that my parents were his parents, as well. They weren't grandparents to him, they raised him. Like myself, my dad taught him how to work, and stay out of trouble. He taught Eric how to cut grass, and grow up to be an extraordinary human being. He succeeded, and if my parents needed anything when he was of age, Eric was always there.

Chapter 8

Eric grew up to be maybe around six foot. He was not scrawny by any stretch of the imagination. I will admit, he had one of the most docile attitudes of anyone I knew. He always dressed nice with button-up shirts, ironed pants, nice shoes, and a matching belt. He smelled of cologne everywhere he went, and his hair was always cut. He had sarcasm, and jokes for days. There weren't many things that bothered him, or at least if they did, you couldn't tell.

In the detached room in my parents' backyard, that's where he lived. He would go to work almost every day for long hours. In his free time, if he were home, I would go knocking at his door to see if I could watch whatever scary game I was too afraid to play myself. He would let Peewee, the dog, in that room, because my mom was often very against having dogs in the house. By this time, Peewee was no longer all black. He was black, gray, and white. He had a floppy ear, and he was beginning to lose teeth. He sat there comfortably on Eric's couch, with his tongue hanging out of the side. Like myself, Eric had a soft spot for that

dog. He was there during both of our childhoods, so it was nat-
ural that we treated him like the family he was.

I know that Eric, in particular, didn't have the easiest childhood. I know that his own father wasn't around, and when I
was a teenager, he would explain that he didn't quite have one
with his mother, either. He would say that she just wasn't there
for him, and even though he loved her, he considered my parents
to be more like his parents. Besides getting his behind handed
to him, I believe by our conversations, that he just didn't feel
the love that his younger siblings would receive. He was never
the apple of his mother's eye, and even though he never said
outright that it hurt his feelings, my habit of absorbing everyone
else's feelings said otherwise. Despite the way he grew up, I can
say that he turned out to be an amazing human being. Besides
my dog, he was truly my best friend.

I believe that some of the biggest hurt I knew about that he
carried was something having to do with his younger sister. She
went off and did positive things with her life straight out of high
school. Eric supported her, because that was his little sister. He
wanted to be a support system in her life. Now, when I tell you,
this girl had the attention of the majority of our family, I'm not
exaggerating. I have never physically witnessed the immense ass-
kissing to one person like I did around this time. Sometimes, I
still do.

For clarification, many referred to her nickname, Princess. I
hope that tells you something. I, myself, never quite had a relationship with her. I don't personally know her, and back in the

day, I didn't have enough in common with her to form a conversation. However, I do not believe that she wanted all of this outward attention from family. Maybe she did. When people spoke about her, it was everyone bragging for her, instead of her doing it herself.

When she graduated high school, she left as soon as I believed she possibly could. She left for the military, and I recall that the bulk of our family went to see her when she graduated. Of course. It's a big deal, and you have to have people there to support your accomplishment. Give this some time, and she became successful in this occupation, and in her own right. From afar, I am proud of her. The wasps that surround her are too much for me to try, and attempt to be a part of her life. I know that if I try, I will eventually be stung.

Eric had a relationship with her, but not as strong as it could've been. I know that they eventually had a falling out over a loan. He had borrowed money from her, and something imploded. As hard as Eric worked, he didn't have a high school diploma, or a GED to serve him in the workforce. Every job he got, he started at the bottom, and worked his way up to the top. I'll give him credit, he had nothing handed to him, and he tried. However, all I can gather is that he wasn't able to pay her back the loan, and their relationship fell through. At least in his eyes, and that was one part of a grown man's broken heart.

Chapter 9

In his younger days, Peewee would get in trouble. When my dad would go to the backyard door and open it, he would run inside, and head straight underneath my dad's bed. When we all would run to see what happened, we'd find a giant blackbird that he killed, and left under my dad's bed. Thank goodness for home movies, because it was recorded the times that Peewee would completely harass my niece. She would hang out with me at the house, and watch cartoons in the living room. My niece carried around this white teddy bear, dressed in a floral dress, and a bow.

She carried that thing around everywhere, but when we got into our cartoons, nothing else existed. So, Peewee would sneak around, grab the doll, and run away with it. He hopped on top of the seat back of the sofa, and treated that doll either like his girlfriend, or like his own personal chew toy. It was all fun, and games until the doll's head got ripped off. Then it was pure chaos.

I'm not sure why he bothered my niece so much. He chased her in the house, grabbing onto her clothes. If she fell, or was in reach, he would pull her hair. She would shriek, and cry, because he just wouldn't leave her alone. On my end, it was just plainly funny. Peewee never harmed a hair on my head, so for him to act like a lunatic and watch my dad chase him, because he was chasing her, was something that looked to be from the circus.

He wasn't feeling that young anymore. Candy, the other chihuahua, was no longer there anymore to keep him company, as she died in her sleep on the porch of the doghouse some time back. I was too young to know then, but I don't think she was in the best of health. I loved her; I just don't remember very much about her except that she was the mother of multiple litters. That, and she was Peewee's only buddy. Besides her, he hated any other dog. Male, or female.

My mother, surprisingly, took me one day to go look at chihuahua puppies. Of course, I was excited. My mother always wanted one of those tiny, teacup chihuahuas with the little apple heads. I laugh, because to me they look like tiny aliens, but to each their own. I remember there being two puppies left in this man's living room, and I don't recall the criteria I held these puppies to, but I made my pick, and named her Princess.

Oh, when I tell you that she became my dog, it would be an understatement. She was all tan, tiny, and extremely smart. She fit in both of my hands, she followed me everywhere I went, and in the car, she would make her comfy spot on my shoulder. Every day I placed her on top of an old desk we had, and would teach her all the simple commands. When she got those down pat, we got roll over, fetch, speak. I even got extra creative as a young teenager, and taught her to annoy my mother by pushing her bedroom door open, and to "pick-pocket" dollar bills out of my dad's pants pocket. He usually left his work pants in reach, and the wallet sticking out of the back pocket. It got to the point where when it came time to wash Princess' bed, you'd find dollar bills underneath her toys.

Funny enough, she got much bigger than anyone expected. My mother was so unhappy that she paid a lot of money for a teacup chihuahua, and we got this sausage with legs. It was too late, though, because that was my baby. She was the only other dog to get along with Peewee, and they were just two peas in a pod. I'm glad that she was there, because as Peewee got older, he developed glaucoma in both eyes, deafness, and was losing his teeth. Snaggle-tooth was more like it. We couldn't rearrange the backyard when he became an old-timer. He couldn't see, and so if we moved anything, he'd bump right into it. Food time required banging the metal bowl on the concrete so that he could hear it, and he enjoyed being picked up like a baby, and wrapping his paws around my arm.

When I was in high school, I worked as a veterinary assistant in an animal hospital two minutes from my parent's house. Princess would go with me every day, be the honorary representative when clients walked in, and then we would go home. While I worked there, I had Peewee there, and they found a tumor behind his eyeball. There was no other treatment except to remove the eyeball, and so after that he had a permanent wink. That didn't stop him from doing anything, and so I believe we had prolonged his life, or marginally increased his quality of life in doing that surgery.

It couldn't have been more than a couple of years when my mother called me at work one day. She said Peewee was screaming, and crying, and they couldn't figure out why. I rushed home, and when I got there, I could barely pick him up without just wailing out in pain. When I arrived back at work, the vet looked him over. I can't reiterate back to you the diagnosis, but I do remember that I was advised that he wasn't going to get better, and his quality of life was at an all time low.

That hit me hard, because that was the first best friend I ever had. We were always together, and that dog loved me as much as I loved him. So, for me to hear that he was in pain, and suffering, I had such a heavy heart that it hurt. I took him outside in the yard where it was warm, and I sat on the concrete, and just held him tight while I waited for the vet to set up for the euthanasia. He cried, and cried. I couldn't budge without hurting him, but he didn't let go of my arm, and I didn't let go of him.

The vet came outside, and offered to do it there, so that we wouldn't have to move. She sat down in front of me, and set two syringes on the floor. One sedative to help him relax, and the other unmistakable bright pink syringe. If you've ever been present while having a pet put down, you know what I'm talking about. Looking down at him, he was no longer my "baby." He lived a long life, and even though it was him, and not me, all the memories I had of him rushed through me. He was my old man, my best friend for all those years. He earned every good thing he ever experienced.

When she gave him the sedative, he cried, and I cried, but the bond that we had, I knew my best friend's time had come. I couldn't be selfish, and try to keep him for myself. That wouldn't be right, and as much as I would miss him, I knew that I couldn't ask for him to stay any longer. I finally realized that the pink syringe was still in her hand, but that he was no longer breathing. I think us being together one last time was enough to let him know that it was okay; that he could move on. That's what I believe, because at that moment I knew my best friend was ready to go, and forever he would be gone. All it took was being in his favorite place—which was in my arms—and he could fall asleep peacefully for good. That dog gave me more than 16 years of his life, and I will cherish him for the rest of my life.

We walked back inside, so that I could put him in one of the rooms. When I set him in there, and turned around to walk out, Princess was in the doorway with her head cocked to the side. If my heart weren't already torn in two, it was then. People say that animals don't feel sadness, or heartbreak. I don't think that's true at all. I think pets mourn the ones they love, just as we do. I think that I was right in giving Princess a moment in that room, and when we went home that day she wasn't the same. Letting her into that backyard was disheartening, because she no longer had her friend to greet her. I believe they feel it all.

Chapter 10

When I became a teenager, I emotionally imploded. At the time, I believed it to be teenage hormones. I figured that no teenager really got along with their parents. I loved my father to pieces. I was daddy's girl, but that didn't stop us from bumping heads constantly. I wanted to become more independent, but my father strongly opposed that change. I had "boyfriends," and I believe as any typical father, he was extremely against relationships. I wanted to purchase my first car, and that was an issue, as well. Perhaps, because they were old-fashioned, he would've preferred that I not work, and have someone else support me, but that was never in the cards for myself, and it caused friction in our relationship.

Teenage life was...interesting. That family mystery I mentioned to you earlier was still amidst until one day. I was in my bedroom scrolling through Facebook on my laptop. I had received a notification from a name I didn't recognize. Cindy. It was a message, and as I read through it, I could feel my face become tense. Basically, she told me that she was my real mother, and that since my parents wouldn't tell me, she took it upon herself to be the one to break the news.

She wanted to get to know me, and that she had this seemingly fulfilled life now that she wanted to share with me. I wasn't confused, and I wasn't relieved. I was pissed. As I said, from a young age, I had a hunch things weren't exactly as they seemed. I knew there were probably other people involved—I just didn't know who, but here she was basically sticking her nose in my life, and I felt angry. When I was trying to figure things out, I told myself that no matter what I found out about my life, I would never feel differently about my parents. My actual parents.

I messaged her back letting her know that I had no interest in a relationship, and her response leaned on the side of surprise. I doubled down, and I deleted her message. She never tried to get a hold of me after that. I did go to the kitchen right after that, and mentioned it to my mother. Then, I went to my father's bedroom, and told him. The consensus I received was that this woman was nuts. That answer felt humorous, and while I knew that wasn't the truth, I never inquired about this woman again.

Between both parents, I had on and off relationships with both of them. They were very seldom on the same page of how to raise me. To make things worse, it wasn't just myself against my parents, it was my parents against each other. I never saw a healthy relationship, or marriage when I was growing up. My parents were constantly calling each other vulgar names. My mother would tell my dad to leave, and be with his "other woman," my father was cussing her up, and down over "her" family, or they would meet in the middle, and argue about money. Lucky me, I heard it all.

The rest of my family, I never saw healthy, conducive relationships. They were either short-lived and onto the next one, or they had the same negative habits of my parents. I've seen some of my family members just in it for the money, and I've seen family members that were just plain undeserving. So, I decided rather than waiting for someone to teach me what to do in my life by example, I would take all of their unintentional lessons, and teach myself all the things to not do.

I will say that one of the things that bothers me the most was how much I fought with my father when I was a teenager. We went at it like our lives depended on it to where I started showing signs of distress at school. I talked to my guidance counselor multiple times as if he were my therapist, and the biggest thing I feel I ever told him was that I loved my father, but I did not like him. Thinking back, that was probably true in the moment in terms of how I felt, but not years later. Not now.

I remember the point when I was about 20, and I was working, and was a student at the local community college. My father and I weren't on the same page at all, and we weren't on speaking terms. It must have been weeks, and in the time I was working and being a student, I was setting myself up to get ready to join the military. I had been working out, and planning out the little details of my life at home. When the actual time came, I remember getting a ride to the hotel where a transportation service would pick myself, and many others, up to go to our next destination for processing. When the car door opened, my father was there. He leaned in the car, and gave me the tightest hug I ever had, and he wept as if someone had passed. It hurt. My father was not a crying man. As loving as he was, he was not the coddling type, and it was rare that he admitted he was wrong, but as much as we argued, I never doubted this man's love for me.

I will forever have the memory burned into my subconscious. Besides when my uncle had passed, I hardly ever saw my father cry. At that moment, I knew he felt bad about all the time we wasted not getting along. So did I, because while the good-bye wasn't forever, we were out of time to hash out all of our issues that we were crying over. I left that day, and a lot of it is a blur. He raised me to be a strong, independent woman. Exactly the way he raised me, I never relied on anyone. He just didn't realize that it was going to include him.

In that car, I wasn't an adult. I was his baby, his daughter, or *mija*. I was so proud to be this man's daughter, and all I ever wanted to do was make him proud. This step, though, wasn't just for me, or him. When I joined high school, I was in the JROTC. As soon as I learned more about the specifics of the military, I was sold. I wanted in, and I can remember for years that I have always had a strong sense of country. This was bigger than me. If you're from Texas, you'll especially know the pride that resonates in its residents. This was just on a bigger scale for me, and no one's words could persuade me to step off this course. Even my father.

My following memories are crammed together, but overall positive. I did weeks of basic training with people I don't know, in a place I had never been in, and striving to just not fail. My parents constantly sent me mail. Even my mother had inked Princess' pawprint on a letter they sent me. I don't recall getting mail from anyone else, but I was hopeful. I did well in basic training, and at one point I surprised T.I.s, or Technical Instructors, because of my blatant honest—-even if I knew there would be repercussions. I kept my head down, worked hard, did my job, and just focused on getting to the next phase.

Before I knew it, I was at my graduation. I was so excited to be done, and when everything was getting prepped, I stood with my group at a standstill in the blazing heat. I stood in the second row with my eyes fixated in front of me, but then I saw a familiar face in the crowd of civilians. Eric. He was looking around, and while I wasn't sure if it were me he was looking for, in my mind I was screaming, "I'm over here! Look, damn it!" He evidently didn't hear my imaginary screaming, and walked off. You don't know how nice a hug sounds until you go months without it. Maybe it's just me, and on the inside, I'm a sap for familiar hugs.

When the entire ceremony was said, and done, I found my people. When I say, "my people," I say that, because the three of them—my mother, father, and Eric—never let me down. I realize that everyone has issues with loved ones at different points in their lives, but besides those, they always tried, and in my most important moments in life, they were there for me. If you remember what I mentioned earlier about my "Princess" niece having a couple of handfuls of support at her graduation, this was not the case for me. That's when I really learned about quality, not quantity. On a good note, I had a pass after graduation, when you're allowed to go with your visitors to eat, or sightsee. We got to my family's hotel room, and to my greatest delight, there was Princess, waiting patiently in the room for someone to come back. I don't know if she, or I was more excited to see the other, but I'll say Princess since she had the wagging tail to prove it. So, let's make that team of supporters into a team of four.

Chapter 11

Time passed, and I went through technical school, where they teach you the job that was assigned to you, and after the fact, you are assigned to a different duty station of Uncle Sam's choice where you then take up residence. Lucky me, in terms of playing roulette with the choices of places to be stationed next, I got what my peers called, "The Black Hole," because once you went there, you never left. Only being in New Mexico, things could've been worse—I think. I was within driving distance if I wanted to visit home, and on paper it didn't seem like it was going to be that bad.

After I graduated from tech school, I went home to visit, and also to get my car and whatever else I was finally able to take with me. Unfortunately, at that time I couldn't take Princess. Pets weren't allowed in the barracks, or what you would consider to be dorms. I knew that it was going to be some hours' worth of a drive, and when I finally got ready to start to pack up my car, Eric had some baggage, also. Unbeknownst to me, he volunteered to drive me to New Mexico to make sure I got there safely. My heart swelled. We made it all the way there without issue, lots of jokes, snacks, and gossip. A short drive away, I dropped him off at the airport, and made my way to my new life.

Little did I know, I would uncover things about myself that not even I knew. When I lived in my barracks room, I lived by myself. Most would call that lucky, and for the most part it was. The small part of me said this was not lucky, because the trouble I had sleeping when I was younger was beginning to become problematic once again. I was hearing things, resulting in unrestful sleep, or hardly any at all. I felt uneasy, and distracted, and in my line of work, that could cause some serious issues, or bodily harm.

When I got settled into this new place, new work, and new co-workers, there was still something I was missing. It wasn't long before I developed a support system from the people that I worked with. That included a soft suggestion from my chain of command to go to mental health services, and talk to a therapist. I was confused. There was nothing wrong with me...right? I said I would think about it, but at the time, that's all I did.

Unfortunately, I came across the man that would become my first husband. The honeymoon stage was long-lasting at first, and I thought this was it. I thought that this relationship would be my last. When I first told my parents about this whirlwind relationship, they weren't exactly thrilled. I hadn't been with this man long at all before we got married, and then moved in together. The disapproval didn't have to be spoken. I already knew, but like most people, I thought that I knew better.

I didn't. I didn't know better. When this relationship started, something inside of me broke. I was so emotionally spun out that I had my work send me to a mental hospital that wasn't too far away for suicidal ideations. I admitted to them that I didn't want to be alive, and that all the people around me would be better off without me, but why? I was in a relationship with someone that I was supposed to be happy with, so why wasn't I happy?

I was driven a couple of hours away to this hospital. It wasn't the best, but thinking back on it now, I was comfortable there. Everyone in my group was a military member in some way. I fit in well, and actually had a decent time when I was in their care. Everyone's story was different, but everyone else in that room understood. With doctors and nurses on staff, the daily routine was pretty much the same. I found out here after weeks of therapy that I had major depressive disorder and anxiety. They worked out some more therapy for me, medications to start on, and I was to continue it all when I got back.

I did just that. I started with a therapist, and continued the medications I was on. Of course, if you've been in a similar situation, you know that medications are trial and error. One pill doesn't work the same for everyone. Not too long after that, I got married to my first husband, and things steadied for a bit. I had some interesting side-effects, but nothing terrible.

This marriage was okay. I tried to have as much of a normal, married life as possible, but it wasn't until roughly a few years later that we were moving back to my hometown. One of my regrets is getting married in the first place. There were a couple of silver linings, but overall, if I could've had those same linings elsewhere, I would have preferred that. I found out through counseling, and a lot of self-reflection, that I got married so quickly was, because of the simple fact that I didn't want to be alone. If it were anything like my childhood, I didn't enjoy the idea of not having someone to talk to.

I wouldn't say that I've always been alone, because that's not necessarily the case. I've had best friends growing up, but we drifted apart. Only one was consistent. I had co-workers, and my parents, silly "relationships," but I didn't have substantial family relationships, or anything else that helped me feel complete. This relationship, this marriage, did more harm than good. The one thing all of my relationships had in common was that they all held secrets.

Chapter 12

After we packed up our home, and began to drive out of that state, I drove my truck, and my then-husband drove his. I had Princess riding shotgun (in case you were wondering), and I let my left hand rest on my months old, pregnant stomach. By that time, we had acquired two new dogs, who sat in the back seat of the other truck. One brindle boxer named Dixie, and a blue-heeler named Maggie who we got as a puppy from a man on the side of the road who just wanted to get rid of her.

Going down that road, I knew I would miss New Mexico. Sure, there were more cows than people, and tumbleweeds that would block roads at times, and dirt that was impossible to keep out of your home, no matter how much you swept it out, but New Mexico for me was more than that. For me, it wasn't the person I was with, but just what I got to experience. There were so many dirt roads, and I had a blast going down them in my truck. I always hoped it would rain, because that was a whole different experience. At night, when you went down those roads, you could see all the stars you wanted, and shooting stars were a little more common.

It wasn't a metropolitan area, that's for sure. The only mall in town everyone called, "The Hallway," because the building stretched into a literal hallway of stores. There wasn't very much green in terms of landscaping, and if you wanted to go anywhere remotely exciting you would have to drive a few hours. It doesn't sound great, but every so often we'd drive to a small town about an hour away. They had car shows and rodeos. The small neighborhood market had their self-grown produce, including watermelons that were sweeter than anything in your local grocery store.

How do I put this? This part of my life, while I hate it the most, it's not the worst thing that's ever happened to me. It was partly my fault, though. I told you I was going to be transparent, and I will. I've had good intentions with almost every decision I've ever made, but that doesn't make them right. I've done a lot shit things in my life, and at the time, I wasn't sorry. I've given my body to men I should have never looked twice at, and that's including my first husband. This man was married, and while I never figured out if it were a sham or not, I had no business befriending someone—especially someone that I learned had feelings for me. I had no business smiling in that woman's face, and I had no business being the reason that their lives became uprooted. That was my fuck-up. In that situation, I was the home-wrecker, and I was the one that thought I was getting a good deal out of it. Needless to say, I wasn't.

What a joke. No, no, let me take that back. I was the joke. That's a part of my life that I'm not proud of. Like I said, I've made more mistakes than I could possibly count. I carry that guilt even until now, and that was years ago. The funny thing is that I spoke to her not too long ago. Months after I divorced him, I was e-mailing back and forth with his ex-wife, and it turns out that she was much happier without him. She had moved back overseas with her two daughters to be with the rest of her family. She told me that he put no effort in keeping in touch, or getting to know them. He paid her one child support payment, and that she didn't care. She was so okay with him not being in any part of their lives, that she wasn't even asking for the money that was rightfully hers. I didn't blame her. She said that she didn't hate me, or wish harm upon me. Her only advice: "Keep him away from your daughter."

Chapter 13

*L*et's get back on track. I worked at a different animal hospital when I got back to Dallas. While it was beginning to look like I was smuggling a small beach ball in my shirt, I believe I held up pretty well. It had only been a short time since I had been back home. I was trying to get a sense of a routine, and a day came where a co-worker yelled from the front of the clinic that someone was on the phone for me. It was my father.

It didn't sound like my father, though. I mean, I knew it was him, but he was crying and wailing. He couldn't get out any words, and it frightened me. I thought something had happened to my mother, and he didn't confirm, or deny. In the middle of his crying, I hung up, and ran out of work. I left, and hauled to parent's house. I was terrified that the day I dreaded most as a kid had finally come. I could barely drive, as I couldn't see through the tears in my eyes.

When I got to my parent's house, I made a beeline to the front door, and when I got inside my father was sitting on the couch still crying uncontrollably. I grabbed his arm, and tried to get some type of answer out of him. My mother's bedroom door was closed, and I was afraid to open it, for I had no clue what may lie inside.

"Dad, what happened?! Is it Mom?!" I screamed at him.

I heard only one name in the midst of the crying and mumbling.

"Eric."

Chapter 14

I knew what death was. I didn't before, but I sure as Hell did when he spoke that name. I stood up in the middle of their living room, and when I turned around, my mother was standing there. I gave her a hug, and at that moment I talked to God. I'm not ever sure who I'm talking to when I have conversations. They could be just to myself, or perhaps this higher power I do have an occasional conversation with is hearing me out. What I do know is that everyone has a fate, and there is little that can be done to keep it from coming.

I didn't cry that day. Actually, I don't remember crying for a very long time. I didn't let it all out—I couldn't. I was numb, and I couldn't find much joy in anything. Even the upcoming arrival of my daughter. Who was going to be there for her if not me? If not Eric? Just like other heavy events in my life, I pushed out a lot of the necessary details to make this into a well-written passage. Let me try to explain.

Eric had many girlfriends in his lifetime. He was good-looking, put together, charismatic, and funny. Along with a million other redeeming qualities. When I got married, Eric wasn't a fan of my husband. Go figure. We, to my deepest regret, had a falling out. Nothing ugly was said, and we never said anything to each other that we would come to regret. For that, in the least I am grateful. I say this, because we weren't entrenched in each other's lives as we once were. I didn't personally know his girlfriends, and I didn't tell him about my marriage. Here, and there, we would message each other, and he would call me "sis." He had said when I got a house, he would build a greenhouse for me. I would rather not have a greenhouse anymore.

His last girlfriend, I came to find out, was not well-liked by family. That is excluding my parents, as far as I knew. This didn't sway my opinion on this unknown woman, because I always felt like I didn't have much of a family to begin with. I always told myself that if they didn't at least like me as a child, they didn't have the capacity to really know me, and perhaps not have such a good judgement of character to begin with. I didn't know this woman, but I found out later it was more than character that made my other family dislike her.

I found out shortly after his death that on a night that it was storming in Dallas, Eric had allegedly gotten into an argument on the phone with this woman. It was supposedly an argument that she wanted to go out, and he did not. Tempers flared, and it escalated. Of course, no one was actually witness to this, so it's all speculation. What isn't speculation is that he got into his SUV, sped down the road, and at some point, he lost control of his vehicle resulting in the driver's side of the vehicle becoming wrapped around a tree in the median. He died on impact.

Everyone attended his viewing, and his burial. Many had the colors of the great Superman, which was the nickname we used for Eric, because of his size, and strength. I didn't feel completely hopeless until I walked up to that casket being a month away from giving birth to my daughter. When I sat back down, the room was full of people I either didn't know, or that I hardly knew—that was family included. I may be alone here, but I have always figured that viewings and all that were for the living. I think that they're the place that living comes to, and gives their apologies for being a shitty person while the deceased were still alive.

Too much? I'm not really sure. You probably think I'm the biggest a**hole you've read a book from, but we can talk it out later. I have come to find out that while I may be a big empath, and I cry over what seems to be the strangest things, I don't cry when it would be socially acceptable. I think I shed only a handful of tears at that funeral. We were in a good place when he passed. We didn't have bad blood, and we didn't talk about each other. There was nothing material of his that I wanted, even after death. I wasn't going to fight with anyone over his belongings. Those things weren't going to bring him back.

That wasn't the same mindset that everyone had. I remember that shortly after he passed, the family beehive was stirring with accusations, anger, and that hive wanted a scapegoat. What does every hive have? You guessed right. Every hive has a queen, and in this hive, it was his mother. This turned from bickering, to a straight-out grudge that was held well over a year, between "The Queen" and our own mother.

There were accusations swirling around our big family that Eric's girlfriend was the reason for his death—that she was the reason he got in that car, and sped off like a bat out of Hell. If it weren't for her, they thought, he would still be here right now sharing laughs. This confuses me, because before his death, I never really saw anyone reach out to him for a catch-up session. He rarely said that he hung out with people, especially family, and now that he was gone, everyone had an opinion on his life. And his money.

When Eric passed, it became public knowledge very quickly that he had a life insurance policy, and that policy went to none other than his girlfriend. In my opinion, who am I to disagree with who he wanted to leave his money to? His possessions? I'm not anyone, in that regard. I don't think anyone is. To make matters worse, he had a little money left in some account. Which somehow, some way, went to my mother. I want to believe that it was, because she always acted like a mother to him, but I never would know for sure. Anyhow, this small amount of change put such a wedge between "The Queen" and my mother that they didn't speak to each other for months. I think blood becomes a little thinner when greed is involved.

Chapter 15

I went to the hospital nearby to have my daughter. My parents, my go-tos in that way, were there almost the whole time I was admitted. I can proudly say that I was one of the quietest women on the maternity floor due to my high tolerance for pain. I strategically waited until about the last hour for the good medications, and before I knew it, there she was. "Little Me." One of two of the best things to come out of that marriage sat there in her tiny clothes, ready to see what life would bring for her next.

When I was home, my feelings weren't right. I was more depressed, and lonelier, and more anxious than I had ever been. I didn't feel like I was going to do right by her. I went back to my OB-GYN, and she told me I developed postpartum depression. If I could accurately describe this to you, I'm sure it would be a lot more helpful. What I can describe was not being able to develop a bond with daughter immediately after she was born. I wanted to be a mother, and I was happy that she was there. At least, deep down I was.

On the surface of postpartum depression, I was sad, and I would cry, and I would become overly anxious to my daughter's cries. I couldn't sleep, and would only find relief if she were with one of my parents, or her dad in another room. I felt so empty, and I couldn't even describe why. When I had gotten back to Dallas, I never found a new therapist. I thought that I was okay, because the years prior to that being back home, I had stayed in therapy continuously. I was happy, but all of that work I had done was erased when I looked in that casket at my "Big Brother." My immediate dreams and aspirations disappeared. I think that the mourning I was doing on the inside was contributing to my postpartum. I didn't want any relationships anymore. Why get attached when there's a chance that one day they'll disappear? My daughter didn't deserve that. She deserved a healthy mom that had her shit together, and that was happy.

It wasn't too much longer after she was born that I realized I didn't want to be like my parents. My now-ex and I had been fighting so much that I constantly imagined just shaking him, and calling him every name I felt was right. The big check the military gave him was supposed to be long lasting. He had spent a lot of that money on his own personal debt, and a few gifts for myself, but that still left a large amount of money unaccounted for. When I asked what happened to the money, I never got a straight answer.

After receiving many lies, and contradicting stories about menial things, I was fed up. I didn't want my daughter to experience what I did being in a broken home. I wanted her to see her parents in healthy relationships, and happy, and setting a good example for her. I was not going to be one of those people that stayed in a toxic relationship for the sake of not having a split home. No. Perhaps others could make those situations work, but I could see her in my shoes in my imagination, and it would terrify me. Shortly after this realization, I was done. I told him that I wanted a divorce, and he needed to find somewhere else to go.

We agreed on a couple of things pending our divorce. One was that we would coparent, and secondly, our daughter would live with him pending my return to therapy, and getting myself back on track. This prompted his mother moving, for the second time, to help him out. She packed her belongings, and moved to the unfamiliar Dallas to help her son, and her newborn granddaughter. I say she helped him, but she helped me, too. She had a hand in raising my daughter for the first couple of years. For the time being, everything was good. We lived in separate apartments no more than a few miles apart, and would share her birthdays, and Christmases, and other special events so that she would see us in the same room. Yes, things were good in that moment, but all good things come to an end.

Chapter 16

I had decided somewhere in my life between my daughter being born, and my divorce, that I wanted to follow in my father's footsteps. I wasn't sure what I wanted to do in my life as far as a career, but the only other good thing my ex-husband did was suggest that I go to school to be an automotive technician, and see how I liked it. I called my dad right after the conversation, and told him about the idea. He was elated that I wanted to be just like him, and that he was proud of me.

So, I did. I began school, balancing it with my first job in the automotive field, and motherhood. I wish I could tell you this is where my feel-good life began, but I would be lying to you. I haven't lied yet, so I'm not going to start now. If you're wanting to read a happier story, I suggest this is where we part ways, or maybe skip to the end.

Everything started out like everyone's relationships. People meet, and go through the honeymoon stage. This was exactly like that, but the rest of it was a crock. When I met the man in this relationship, I was confident, and bold, and self-assured. I felt good about myself. He was much older than me, and at the time it didn't matter. "Age is just a number" crap. I met him at my first job, and from the get-go, like other times, people told me to leave that man alone, he wasn't what I thought, etc.

I dated this man for a while, but it wasn't too long before he moved into my apartment with me. I lived only a few minutes from work, and things were going well. I should have realized that something was a little off when he would show signs of either insecurity, or secrecy. I had purchased a new sectional couch one day, and when it was going to be delivered, I had a friend help me lug it up the flight of stairs so that it would be a surprise. Or so I thought.

When he arrived home his face wasn't that of surprise, or gratitude. It was questions scattered all over his face. He sat down with me, and the first question that he had was who helped me get it up the stairs. I laughed, because I didn't think it was that serious, and my response was, "I think you mean to say, 'Thank you.'" There were other instances that didn't sit well with me, but I guess my hopeless romantic side overshadowed my common sense.

We began to fight, because I started to feel like he was hiding things from me. If you knew me, you would know that I'm a very understanding person. I would prefer that you hurt me with the truth, than try to protect me with a lie. So, when I found out the first time that he was staying up past when I would go to bed to talk to his own ex, it ticked me off. Of course, instead of owning up to it, or talking it out with me in a reasonable way, he would either blame me, or he would call it quits right then, and there, and leave to move back in with her.

This happened a couple of times, and I blame myself for allowing him back in my door. A good portion in, I didn't have a good support system anymore, or the little that I did have prior. I had kept my dogs, Princess and Dixie, from the divorce before I had this relationship. They were the little positive company that I had besides that man. We were no longer getting along by this point, and it started to become heated.

Since there was no trust, being in the same room together was practically unbearable. If we were in public, and we would disagree on a topic, he would become so irritated by just my presence. There was nothing I could say, and if I dared to have tears in my eyes, he would become embarrassed. He would throw money on the table, and rush out, leaving me at the table alone in a room full of strangers. Most of them had looks of pity on their face, and I felt so ashamed.

I would do my own personal walk of shame to the car where he would be waiting, and he would yell at me in the car, curse me, wave his arms. When we would get back to the apartment, if I wanted to make up, he would ignore me. He would have this smug look as he looked on the couch, and would proceed to tell me that I didn't deserve to be held, or shown affection. To just go to bed alone, and cry in there. I had never felt so alone.

I was done seeking affection. That's not the affection I wanted, and that wasn't love. It escalated into pure hate, or at least that's what it felt like. I already had a history of suicidal ideations. I never had a plan, but the thoughts plagued my mind. We had such a huge blow-up that I left work early to avoid him. We texted back and forth, and when I told this man that was supposed to love me that I wanted to die that day, he told me to go ahead and do it.

Chapter 17

It wasn't long into this joke of a relationship that I found out some news about my father. I wasted the time having my parents meet this "man." When I found out that my father was diagnosed with lung cancer, fear struck me. This was a shell of a man that I remember growing up. My father was not the type of man to regularly go to the doctor. He believed he was always healthy as horse, and he felt ill, he would go about his daily routine as if it were the common cold.

He, nor my mother, told me when he first found out. He never told me when things were going on with him, because he never wanted me to worry. I wish that one time that he wanted me to worry. I wanted to know. I would've liked to know about something so heavy. I would've liked more time, but that's my fault, too. I wasted more time trying to fix a broken relationship with a man that didn't care about anyone, but himself. I didn't take the time to go sit with my father, and enjoy the last bit of time that stage four lung cancer would give him.

I thought I caught a lucky break the last time that man walked out on me. I thought that was it. He left, but the damage was done. I couldn't sleep in my own bed after that. That room haunted me. I didn't like looking over at the bathroom, or the closet, where I would hide from him to avoid another fight, or other ways he could list the ways of how I wasn't good enough.

I slept on the couch for months. I would leave the television on, and listen to Anthony Bourdain. He had a softer voice that I could fall asleep to. That was my security blanket for a really long time. I couldn't enjoy my apartment anymore. I hated it. To top it off, I even had a neighbor that turned creepy when he found out I was living alone. He came knocking at my door one night with two beers in his hands, and let himself in. He stayed for ten minutes, or so. He wanted something, but I shot a quick text to my daughter's dad who lived around the corner. I made it apparent I wasn't in the mood for company, and I showed him out as my daughter's dad arrived.

I had gone to my parents' house one day. My father had been wearing various hats on his head to hide his hair loss from my daughter who was about three at the time. One of my favorites was this camouflage hat I remember him wearing to do yard work. I would give him a hard time, and told him I could get him another hat, but he insisted on wearing this one. Now, he was wearing it for a completely different reason, and it pulled on my heartstrings.

He was standing in the kitchen that day. It was a short time until Christmas, and I asked him what he wanted for a gift. It was the typical answer that he would give me, saying that he already had everything that he wanted. He quickly changed his mind, and said that he'd like an aftershave I had already bought him in the past. I laughed, and I told him I would try to find it again for him.

Less than a month later he was in the hospital. His cancer had taken a turn for the worst. When I arrived at the hospital, he was awake, but he didn't look well. I don't remember if it were just that one day, or two, that I went, and we were able to talk. I tried to keep it light, and tell him that we'd be able to play a game of cards soon. He made it a point before I left one day to tell his team of doctors that I was the one to make his medical decisions for him. I know that the next time I went, and he was awake, they had already intubated him, because he couldn't breathe on his own.

I walked in, and held his hand. I tried not to cry, but he was just looking at me, and it seemed like he still had a million things to say to me. I know that he didn't want me to see him that way, and I know he didn't want me to hurt. Even more, he was afraid for my daughter. Just like me, she was his baby. He treated her like a queen, and I know that he wished he had more time. All I could tell him was, "You know I love you, right?" He nodded his head, and his eyes welled up with tears.

Shortly after, my next visit revealed that he was no longer awake. He was put into a medical coma, and that it probably wouldn't be long until he passed. What it also revealed was my "Godly brother" was sitting in the room next to my father's bed. This rubbed me the wrong way like you wouldn't believe. He was asking the medical staff questions, and making requests. They didn't have a good relationship, nor did they ever sit down and have a conversation. So, I found it odd for him to be sitting in that room alone with my father when he finally couldn't speak up for himself.

When it became clear that the only decisions that were going to be made were by me, tensions flared. I remember I went to have dinner with a family member that night, and his wife sent me a text. In a nutshell, it said that if I were going to take charge of my father's care, and well-being, then they, or she was laying claim to our mother, because that was her son, and he should have the right to call the shots if she were unable to for herself.

Part of me was appalled, but another part of me snorted in laughter, because my mother wasn't going to have anyone speak for her as long as she's alive to say anything about it. Even so, I wasn't the type of vulture to try and lay claim on a body that's still warm. I wanted to text back, and ask what was wrong with her, or them, but I know I would just get more BS shoved back my way. It wasn't worth my time, and I took solace in the fact that I bothered someone so much just by my place in the family, and the threat they felt was real to them.

The last time I went to the hospital, I told the doctors that it was time for him to come off the vent. I knew my father, and I knew that if he were going to fight, it was going to be off the machine. If he were going to make it, he was going to do it on his own.

That's the type of man he was. Before they did, I took one last picture of him in that hospital bed with my head on his bedside. I wanted something to show me that I wanted to be there until the end.

Practically everyone in the family was there to pay their respects, and say their good-byes. Besides that day already being the worst day of my life, what made it worse is that while myself, and others stood bedside, my mother sat with her son, and his wife on the sofa to the side of the room. It wasn't just their presence that pissed me off; it was that they were busy talking about how my father should've lived a holier life, and then maybe he would make it to Heaven. They weren't crying, they weren't consoling each other, or anyone else in the room. I am convinced that they basked in the darkness in that room, and they were happy to watch him die, because without him alive to lay down his own law, his home, and the decisions for my mother laid unguarded. Make no mistake, I saw vultures of death sitting in that room. They sat there, and wore masks claiming they spoke the word of the Lord. I will never forget that moment. I don't hate anyone, but they sit extremely close.

My father passed not too long after they transferred him into a hospice room. I said my final good-byes, and I hoped that my mother would let me know not too long after what his funeral arrangements would be. Ha! If only I were so lucky. Originally, when Eric died, he didn't have a plot of his own. I don't know of too many younger people that prepare for their death. So, when he passed, my father forfeited his own plot, so that Eric would have a place of rest.

I know you've heard the saying, "No good deed goes unpunished." He wasn't paid back for this good deed. He was cremated, and scooped into an urn. To pour salt in the wound, my mother didn't even want him. Vicky ended up taking him, and while I was grateful for her doing so, I felt my stomach in knots, because I know that's not what my father would've chosen for himself. He wanted a final resting place, and he got the most convenient choice.

There was a point that I went to my parents' house, and I wish I had gone sooner. It looked like my father hadn't existed at all. His belongings in the house were gone. Clothes, jewelry, photos, files. Gone. I wasn't on the team of my mother at the time. After what I heard in the hospital in that day, I just couldn't look at her, and think, "Poor you." It was like she was glad he was gone. She had always told me and other people that she couldn't wait to have the house to herself. She couldn't wait to be able to do whatever she wanted, and if I didn't believe her then, I did now.

Chapter 18

January 7th was the day my world not only fell apart, but it eroded, imploded, was set aflame. Anything destructive you can think of, I was in the middle of it. I drowned my former self, because the one person in this world that I wished God would make an exception for was gone. It blew through me like a hurricane. All of the memories whipped through my mind, and it was like I was going to experience death for myself.

When we were in that hospital, the hospital staff allowed my then two-year-old daughter to say good-bye to her pawpaw. The only other person besides myself that felt that void was her, and she was a young me when I first experienced death. I felt so useless as I imagine my parents did, but that wasn't an uncle of hers, that was her grandfather. The one man that I knew would do anything for her, and would never allow anyone to disrespect her.

Within the same week, that same piece of garbage man that had walked out before, showed up at my door, and decided he wanted to be there and try again. The verbal and emotional abuse did wait to start. I didn't have time to mourn my father, and I had this worthless man yelling at me, telling me I was the one that wasn't worth a damn. There was no love there. I wanted to be alone, but I had my own personal squatter that said he loved me in his own twisted way. The boiling point was the night we got into an argument over who-knows-what. He didn't want to reconcile that night, and told me to just go to bed. That's what I did. I went to bed facing the wall, and cried myself to sleep. I often took sleep medication to aid my insomnia, so it took me a moment to realize what was happening. Within a few hours of me going to bed, he decided that his way of reconciling with me would be to rape me while I tried to sleep. When I awoke, he had just started, or tried to have sex with me, and I immediately pulled away.

When I did completely come to, I had a meltdown. I was so offended that doing that was his way of apologizing. Not so shockingly, he was angry at me for not being more accepting. I had no emotional fuel after this. I don't remember much, but I do remember that the lease there ended, and he found another one smack dab in the middle of both of our work locations. Becoming emotionally hollow is an understatement. I hated him. I did hate this person.

He had given me fake rings to wear, because he wanted to marry me. That was a lie. At least, I held my breath that it was a lie, because while I wasn't going to be forced into a marriage, I knew that it would be a much easier split if he were the one that decided he didn't want it. I knew in this relationship why people say it's not as easy as you think to escape an abusive relationship. Per statistics, women are 70 times more likely to killed in the two weeks after they leave their abuser. That was one statistic I didn't want to be a part of.

Chapter 19

We ended up moving into that new apartment. I had left Princess with my mom, and had my boxer, Dixie with me. She was on paper my emotional support animal. She went with me many times to complete errands. It wasn't even a few months into living in the new apartment that he pushed me to get rid of her. Instead of dropping her into a shelter, I had one of my co-workers come and pick her up. She hopped in that truck, and I haven't seen her since.

He blamed the fact that she was having accidents for him wanting her gone. While I understand that it's not ideal to have an animal constantly defecating in your space, I believe that the constant fighting between him and me not only stressed her out, but scared her into not wanting to ask in her normal way to go outside. I had her for years before that, and never had a problem with her misbehaving. I was thankful someone I knew was able to take her, and I prayed that she was happier. If I were going to suffer in that situation, she shouldn't have had to, as well.

Flashing back to New Mexico. I was in the market for another dog. I just had Princess there, and I wanted her to have another dog home while I worked. There was a local shelter nearby, and I looked online to see what they had. There was one dog that caught my eye, and I jumped in the truck to head that way. I was so excited for this dog, and I couldn't hide how happy I was to rescue this dog.

Pulling into the parking lot, I hopped out, and saw that there was already a line out of the door. There was a couple standing in front of me, and when they got to the desk, the woman behind the desk ushered them in the direction of the kennels. When I got to the desk, I inquired about the specific dog to her, and she said, "Oh, no. The nice people that were in front of you came to pick that dog up. However, there are many other dogs that you can look at."

I was disappointed. I wanted to go home, but figured since I was already there, that I might as well look at the other dogs. I walked down the aisle of the kennels. So many dogs were hopping on the fence, barking, each one trying to get the attention of the people outside of the gate to find a new home; each one unknowingly trying to get out before their timer hit zero, and they would have to be disposed of to make room for all the other dogs coming in.

I wasn't seeing one that I thought would be a good fit for me, but I turned around to get ready to leave, and I glanced inside this cage that I believed to be empty. It wasn't. There she was, emaciated, skinny, bones showing. She couldn't have pinned herself against that wall any tighter. She was terrified. She had a little bed, and toys, but she looked like she was afraid to breathe.

The kennel person came to take her out, and she didn't want to walk. If my memory serves right, she had to be carried out. When I signed the papers to take her home, she was too afraid to do anything, but as soon as the back door of that truck opened up, she hopped right in. The whole way home that day, she rested her face on the center console, and fell asleep. She was home.

Chapter 20

He had successfully isolated me. I didn't talk to friends; I didn't talk to anyone. I can't say I didn't talk to my family, because there were no relationships there anyways, but my father was gone, and I was with this ass playing house. It did get to the point that I tried to play nice. I tried to be a supportive girlfriend, fiancé, whatever you want to call it. I would just call myself a pawn, but whatever you choose to call me, I'm sure it's fitting.

Things were becoming more strained than usual. I accompanied him to doctor's appointments, and once again, my memory doesn't serve me well in terms of remembering the diagnosis, or the track that the doctors were on. I sat on the side of the MRI machine, and gave him all the support he always refused to give me when I didn't behave the way he thought was appropriate.

Something wasn't right. The time following those appointments, he was abnormally docile. He was fighting less, and I figured he was becoming bored, or lazy. I remember this clearly: I woke up early for work one day, and walked out of the bedroom.

He was sitting on the couch, where he had been sleeping. He had been complaining of back pain—hence the previous appointments, and so he hadn't been going to work. I grabbed my keys, and other items, said "sweet" good-byes to keep him from becoming dissatisfied, and he said that he would see me when I returned from work.

My suspicions heightened when I was at work. All through the workday, he didn't correspond with me, and that was extremely abnormal. I became anxious, and as soon as 5:00 hit the clock, I rushed out of work. When I pulled up to the apartment, his car wasn't outside, and the front door was unlocked. I walked inside, and if you weren't familiar with how the apartment looked, you wouldn't know there was anything different, but me, I have an annoying attention to detail. I don't want to say I notice everything, but I would say that it's pretty damn close.

Things were missing from the living room, and the little belongings that he did have were, also, missing. He had quickly gathered his things when I left for work that morning. For someone that could barely move off the couch, he sure did show himself out with haste. It would've been a glorious moment, except that he chose that apartment. He chose an apartment that had the rent amount that two people should've been paying. Not me alone. I'm not sure if I were more relieved, or furious.

That following week I notified the front office of what had happened. They told me that they could either evict me, or I could break my lease early. Talk about being stuck between a rock, and a hard place. I figured I would give myself some time to figure out my game plan. All the money I had went to the previous apartment, and to moving into this new apartment that I quickly realized was well above my means.

I didn't know what I would do next, and didn't have any favors to pull. Contacts that I had previously, I didn't have anymore. I would do my usual of picking up my daughter, and having her with me for bits at a time. Luckily, she didn't develop a relationship with that man. She only asked about him one time, and she never asked me again. I thought that after this, things would get better. I really have to stop lying to myself like that.

<h1 style="text-align:center">Chapter 21</h1>

I was in the slow process of selling possessions of mine since I was otherwise broke. I would go about my daily routines, and try to stay as level as I could. Every other week-end, I would call my ex-mother-in-law, and asked if she wanted to go with my daughter and me to various places. We would go on day trips, lunch, or I would take them to my apartment to hang out with me for the day.

Things had changed with my ex-husband, and his relationship status. I knew that he was dating a woman when I was in my first apartment. I was glad that he was getting out there, and trying to date around. We were friends back then, and could openly talk about new relationships, and our daughter. Even the lawyer I used for our divorce said that our divorce was the most amicable divorce he had ever worked on. If he asked my opinion on these women, I gave it, and he typically was there for me to chat with if I needed an ear.

The woman I knew he was dating was okay, or so I heard from him. They were on, and off, and there were some differences. The age gap between him, and this woman was a difference of about 11 years, with her being the eldest. She already had four children of her own from previous relationships, so I was surprised that this was who he wanted to make a relationship with. It wasn't my business, and so I did whatever made him happy.

I guess while I was dealing with my off and on relationship, he was dealing with his own. He came to my apartment looking broken-hearted, because she had told him basically that they weren't going to work. She didn't believe that we were over, and her insecurities told her that I was the one he was going to go back to. I scoffed at the idea, but offered to talk to her myself. I told him to call her, and tell her to come over to my apartment.

I wish I hadn't made match-maker that night. Looking back, I should've let it fall apart like it was already. When she arrived that night, she looked...uncomfortable. I invited her to sit down on the couch, and when I tell you that she couldn't sit more on the edge of that couch, I wouldn't be lying. I offered her something to drink, and she declined. My ex waited outside, and I laid it all down on the table. I didn't want him anymore, we co-parent, we're friends, but that's all that it would be. I told her she should give it a chance, and apparently they did.

It wasn't long before his mom told me that they were moving to a large house about an hour away. I let him know that I would stay out of it as long as our daughter was taken care of. As long as he stayed a consistent parent in her life, we would never have any issues. When we divorced, I didn't ask for child support, because at the time, she was living with him. The deal had always been the same. I would never make issues unless he started to lack as a father to our daughter.

They moved into this large house, and I knew right after that our relationship had changed for good. He was so indulged by this new relationship that our daughter was being left in the wind. When my daughter would come to visit me, she would start to misbehave in ways she never had before. By what I got out of her, she wasn't a fan of her dad's new girlfriend. Misbehaving may be the wrong term. She was acting out. I had my first clue when I had my daughter over at my first apartment. I was in the kitchen making her food, and she came in asking for snacks. I knelt down on the floor to explain that I was making food, and she could have snacks later. Her response was to try and slap me across the face.

So, yes, that was my first clue that this relationship of his was going to alter multiple relationships. His girlfriend didn't want him being friends with myself anymore, and that meant co-parenting. Her insecurities were so big, that she wanted everyone else to disappear. Never in a million years did I think he would give up on the relationship with his daughter, but I guess if you're lonely enough, you'll take anything.

Loop back to the second apartment I was getting ready to leave. I received a phone call one evening from his mother. She was crying, saying that she was getting kicked out. I told her to calm down, and I'd be there soon. I drove about 30 minutes to his new house, and he, his mom, and my daughter were standing outside. When I got out, his mom, and my daughter got into the truck, so I could talk to him alone.

He said that they weren't kicking her out, that they were planning to help her find another place to go. I was shocked. I questioned these "plans," asking him how did they figured it would work out to relocate her elsewhere. She lost her car, because of him being in need of money, so she took out a title loan on this already paid-off car. He promised to help her pay it back, and that fell through, so she didn't have transportation. She had already been diagnosed with breast cancer, and had other medical ailments, and even more, she was on a fixed income living in one of the higher cost-of-living metropolitan areas. How in the world did it make sense to stick her in some random place just so that he could make this new woman happy? I was so confused, but I told him that I was taking her in with me, and our daughter was coming with me. This fool had no objections. So, either he just wanted the whole ordeal to be over, or he just didn't give a damn. I knew that financially, it wasn't the smartest idea, but somehow, I was going to make it work. I had to.

Chapter 22

My own mother had been in medical facility long-term some months after my father passed away. I called her, and reluctantly asked if we could stay there. She was more than happy to have me living back home. I didn't feel the same enthusiasm. I ended up losing the furniture I had in the second apartment, because I didn't have a way of getting all the larger stuff out. I lost my bed, a bookcase that my father gave me, my couch, my ottoman that had my Nikon camera in it, and multiple other items. The apartment said that they could no longer get ahold of the runaway kid, and that if they couldn't find him, I would be responsible for all the fees, and unpaid rent.

I focused on the future, and decided I would eat the hit I would get on my credit report. We got settled back in my mother's house, and every now, and then again, I would take off for a drive. That was my stress relief. Music, windows down, just me. On this particular drive, I had the fake rings from that imbecile in my hand. As soon as I crossed a bridge, I rolled the window all the way down, and chucked them into the river. I hadn't smiled so big in ages.

Chapter 23

Most of the stay at my mother's is a blur. It wasn't the healthiest move if we're talking about mental health. The passing of my father had a bigger effect on me than I originally realized. My daughter, and my ex-mother-in-law, and I stayed in my mother's home while she was trying to get herself home. The anatomy of our mingling relationships may seem odd, but they worked very well. I don't know anyone else that lives with their ex-mother-in-law, but we got along for the simple reasons that she stayed out of my business, she didn't try to parent my daughter for me, and she respected me as her granddaughter's mother. She didn't give her opinion if I didn't ask for it, and while I worked, I knew I could trust her to be alone with my daughter. She didn't just act like family; she was family—is family.

My depression was so in the hole, and everything else was falling apart with it. I don't know if a broken heart is an actual thing, but I thought I knew pain when Eric passed. This was a million times worse. The pain began to become so unbearable, I numbed the pain like many other people: Alcohol. I went out as often as I could by myself, and I didn't come home until early in the morning. I went out searching for attention from men that I was all of a sudden lacking. I was the epitome of a woman that had "daddy issues."

This went on for a couple of months, and in the morning I would get up to look at myself in the mirror. I looked into my own eyes, and didn't recognize myself. I felt dirty, I felt that if other people knew what I had been doing that they would think I was a whore, a slut, whatever else you want to call it. More so, I knew if my father were still around, he wouldn't be proud of what I was doing, and I felt ashamed. I felt a very heavy hand of shame. It all came to a screeching halt, and I was so deep in it that it took me being raped a second time by a guy I had only briefly dated. By what I remember, he was an alcoholic with extreme self-control issues. I felt like damaged goods. I thought that I would be so unattractive to anyone else, and that continuing to talk to this man was the right move. Eventually, I saw the error of my ways. Don't ask me what happened, because I couldn't answer you. I know that I sat in my car one night, and cried, and cried. I hit my steering wheel, I screamed. I thought I had already screwed up my chances of being with anyone that was worth a damn, and I thought for sure I had already screwed up my chances of being a good role model for my daughter. I just thought that was the end of the road for me.

Chapter 24

That wasn't true. My mistakes didn't determine my worth. I went through a lot of crap just like most people do. I experienced the side of life no one wants to experience, but I was in my early twenties, and I would start everyday starting to feel like myself just a little bit more. I didn't need anyone. I didn't need anyone's approval. I was going to live my life the best ways I knew how. Every man I had met in that timeframe didn't want *me*. They wanted to pass through, and not have an attachment afterwards. I went through the crap I told you about, to having someone try to roofie my drink one night. I ended up with just being bed-ridden for about three days, but I had a vague idea of what happened. I knew how ugly the world could be to someone that's just dragging themselves through their hardships.

No, screw that. Screw the wolves in sheep's clothing. The family that never called to see if I were alive; the friends that disappeared; the strangers that take the opportunity to screw someone over for their own benefit. I figured if people already disliked me, they wouldn't mind hating me for revamping my attitude, and outlook on life. What did I have to lose? I already lost the most important loved ones that I had. I was already at the bottom. What else did I really have to lose?

When I got my head back on straight, it was like being able to see for the first time. I laid off the alcohol, the going out, focused more on work, and my daughter. My mother had finally come back home. As happy as I was that she was back, her return was like dropping chum in the ocean. The sharks could smell it. I was there in the kitchen, sitting on the counter. My mother's preacher son was there visiting, but he had ulterior motives. He walked up to me, and asked if I would mind if he, and his wife, moved into the house with us. I swear I could feel my brain cringe for a moment, as the idea of sharing a close space with these people was not a pleasant one. I couldn't say much, as it wasn't my house, or my decision. All I left the conversation with, was my only stipulation was to stay out my way, and my business. He agreed, and within a couple of weeks they were moving their stuff in. I have always known that they move around like squatters, because either they can't afford where they stay, or they couldn't agree to stay somewhere, even when the church was footing the bill. He was a preacher, but not full-time all of the time, if you catch my drift. My mother would brag that he would get job offers from different churches, but I never saw anything come for it. He was still a mama's boy that relied on other people to hold him up. I suppose that's how he stayed "close to God." He had other people holding him up.

When they were there, every day I would come home, and something in the house would be different. My parent's belongings would disappear, and their own decor would replace it. They would move things in the kitchen, and add their own tacky utensils. When my little family moved in, my ex-mother-in-law made her home in the detached room from the house. I was fine with that, because that would give her some privacy, and she wouldn't have to feel uncomfortable with other people in the home. The preacher's wife began to befriend her, but it was all a facade. She was attempting to befriend her, because she was sniffing for pills, and she knew exactly who to go after.

I won't drag this portion out. I didn't keep my family there very long. As soon as he appointed himself the financial advisor, I knew it was only going to get worse. His wife called my mother out of her name, he made the house uninhabitable. He wasn't working, and so he lounged on the couch in the living room, so that no one else would. All I could think was that he was piggy-backing off of my father's years of hard work, because if this were years ago, my father would have none of this. He would be damned.

The preacher man was beginning to become ornery. He wanted to be king of this castle, but little did he know, I wasn't going to fight it out with him over material possessions, and mommy's attention. That wasn't my M.O. In comparison, as soon as I could begin to work, I did. I could hold jobs, and I didn't need to ask my mother for a dime. He talked at people, I listened to people. I love the expression, "No one ever learned anything by listening to themselves speak." If it sounds like I hold a grudge, that may be the case. I have always had trouble keeping my opinion to myself, and whatever my words don't say, my face certainly does. So, when he began to become rude and ugly to my ex-mother-in-law, and tried to parent my child, I took it personally. If our history weren't enough for me to dislike him on a deep level, those times were.

It came about that I had to let my mother know that I wasn't planning on staying in her home. By that point, I was doing it more for her, than myself. At that time, I hadn't fully forgiven her yet, but I wasn't going to punish my child for things that she had no control over. She deserved a relationship with her grandma, because at the end of the day, that woman raised me, and tried to give me every opportunity in the world to succeed. I didn't agree with everything she did, or everything she said, because that woman is not perfect, but hell, neither am I.

I'm not sure about all of them, but out of the six children that they raised, I only truly dislike one. You, my reader, must have a good gauge on what kind of person I am. I don't go looking for trouble, but don't rattle my cage. Ignorance is exceptionally annoying to my sensibilities. When you don't have all the information, you choose to open your mouth anyways to further spread ignorance.

Living in my mother's home had the unfortunate circumstances where any visitor could come and go. I adore my privacy. I don't enjoy people I don't care for knowing what I have going on. I won't brag about my finances, and I especially don't confide in anyone about what steps I'm trying to take next. The preacher man had gone to the hospital, and the doctors believed he was on his way out. I had come out of my room one of the days that he was out, and one of his children was there to visit. I believe he was there to say his good-byes.

When he saw me, he asked if I would be going to the hospital to visit his father. I didn't skip a beat when I declined, and it took half a beat for both him, and his pale mother to lecture me on the importance of him being my brother, and how I should go, and whatever other hogwash they attempted to guilt trip me with. I mentioned that I didn't come out to talk to either one of them, but I noticed that the look on his face was just as smug, and condescending as his father. I also wondered if family were so important, how come he didn't say good-bye to my father, his grandfather, when he was on his deathbed? Practically everyone else was there, but he wasn't, and you're going to switch to the other one of your two faces, and guilt me? Well, that shows how much you know me, because guilt concerning other people for me runs rare.

My mother wasn't in agreeance with me leaving, but she knew that after I found out that her son got in my ex-mother-in-law's face, I wasn't going to subject my daughter to the negativity, and I wasn't going to put myself in a position where I could lose my temper. He had the audacity to say that she needed to go, as if it were his house. "She needs to go, but you can stay." Well, thank you for the permission. I'm not sure how it feels to try and take over another man's hard work, but if it were me, I would tuck my face in shame. You don't lay claim to a dead man's property when you didn't attempt it when he was alive. What a coward you must be.

I'm probably sounding like the toxic one now, but rest assured, this whole book is to just blow off steam. This is years of things I've bottled up for the sake of having relationships with my family, but I learned long ago that this particular plan was never going to gain traction. I also want to just put it all out there for you, because I know I'm not the only one that's had a bumpy road, and you have every right to be brutally honest, get it all out, and rise from the ashes. No shame.

Chapter 25

I put myself and my small family into an apartment a city over. I felt relief being in a different environment. I had just gotten into a new job right before making the decision to move. The job changed my life, and I truly believe had it not been for this job, and the people in it, I would still be in an emotional ditch. By the point of this job, I had been an automotive technician for years. I took pride in being a woman, and walking in and doing the same work as my male counterpart. This place really took a leap of faith on me, because I had always primarily worked on domestic vehicles. This was the first place where it flipped, and I was working primarily on foreign makes.

They gave me a chance to show my worth, and I believe I did. I loved working here, because they supported me as part of the teams, I worked well with my co-workers, and they gave me new opportunities to learn more, be better. My work life was good, and I enjoyed it. My management were people I could come to if I needed help, and this was the first time I really knew what a positive support system was.

My daughter's dad was lost at sea, apparently. He saw her once for literally months at a time. I tried to fight him on it, and it did me no good. It didn't improve anything for my daughter, and I knew she was hurting. I had always hoped when I had her that she would have a good father-daughter relationship like I did with my own father. The fact that she didn't have that bothered me to no end. Eventually, after a blow up that he had with his own mother, and then cursing me over the phone, because I didn't see his side of having a new family to be accountable for. He couldn't include our daughter, because that would rub his older girlfriend the wrong way—even if he'll never admit it. I gave him the ultimatum of either being physically present in our daughter's life, or I would take him to court for child support. Which, frankly, I think that's a pretty good deal. I'm friends with a lot of guys that would've chosen to be an active role in their children's lives, but not him. I ended up fighting for child support, and got it. He's been lacking more and more in her life ever since. I didn't realize the changes that would begin to affect me, and how I see myself, and my own family.

I went into work early one morning. I had some time to try and talk to one of my sisters. We weren't talking often, but I tried to call every once in a blue moon. This talk was different, because she began giving me information about my adoption. My adoption. I knew growing up that the pieces of my puzzle didn't quite fit. I knew growing up that there were secrets floating around, and the chances of me being biologically theirs were slim, but to hear it actually come out of someone's mouth just solidified it.

What I gathered not too long after that conversation was that pretty much everyone knew that I was adopted from someone else in my family. Everyone knew, and that answered the question I always had about my "siblings" saying, "My mom." When I said it had intent, and now that I can put it all together, they would say it condescendingly, because they believed they held, or should've held, a place in my mother's eyes than myself. I'm not sure if you would classify this as jealousy, but to say this to someone from a child going forward, I'll let you be the judge.

The man I knew to be one of my uncles on my mother's side was actually my maternal grandfather. Per my mother, he had always wanted to tell me. Everyone had apparently always wanted to tell me, but my father wouldn't allow it. My father didn't want me to know so badly that he literally took that secret to the grave with him. I wasn't angry, and I didn't feel betrayed. I knew my father well, and so my educated guess said that he never wanted me to know, because he didn't want me to think differently of him, or my mother.

I believe it was the same night that I had that conversation, and went to see my mother. She answered her front door, and when I casually brought up the adoption, she looked like she saw a ghost. For once, my mother had nothing to say, but I reassured her that while I knew what the secret was, I didn't think differently of her. She was still my mother, and when I told her my thoughts, she put her hand over her heart, and took a big sigh of relief. I let her know that I had a pretty good idea already, so it wasn't a shock, and that I didn't consider anyone else to be my parents besides them.

She told me in return that the familiar name Cindy was accurate. Biologically, she was my mom, but in my mind, she would never be my mother. She, also, said that she didn't know who my biological dad was, and she didn't know of anyone who did. All she remembered was that it was some man back then that was going to college, and when he found out his woman was pregnant, she was no longer his woman. Rumor is that she was not only a stripper, but she was also a drug addict. Her drug habit ran so bad that when I was born, they had to keep me in the hospital to detox me off of her smack. My mother said that I was stuck in that incubator for weeks, and I was too tiny to be taken out.

I was confused when she asked me if I wanted to talk to my bio mom. I straight out said, "No," and she looked just as confused as me.

"You don't want to get to know her?" she asked me.

I explained that I had absolutely no interest in getting to know this woman. The people that knew my bio mom better said she cleaned up her act, but that made no difference to me. All I know up to this point is that she made poor decisions, and while I'm sure she gave me up with the best intentions, or at least I hope she did, I'm already an adult, and I had amazing parents that I know for a fact did everything with my best interests in mind. I am convinced that I had the best chance at life because of them, and I didn't need complete strangers to add to my life to make it worthwhile.

Chapter 26

You always think things can't get worse, except when you realize that the world never stops spinning, aging. Much like ourselves, we go through life with so much haste, trying to reach the next stone to step on, it isn't until we stop for a moment that we see how much we've missed. I guess that's why I never miss a chance to snap a photo. That's the only way I know to capture a moment in time, and that way it doesn't age or die; if we blink for a second, it's not lost forever.

For me, when I finally stopped, Princess was no longer the tiny puppy that used to sleep on my shoulder. She had a white face, and was slow to move. She was much older now. All these years, she spent being my other best friend besides Peewee; all these years she spent giving me unconditional love, even when I didn't know how to give it myself. She was smart, and she made me laugh. I knew that when I took a shower, she would be sleeping in front of the door waiting for me to come out.

We were a team, her and me. Such a little dog with such a big personality. I was finally getting my life together, and I noticed that her ageless face in my eyes was tired. She had developed a small lump on her neck. I knew not to panic right away. Past experiences told me to keep an eye on it, and not to panic unless it grew in size, or became painful for her. My heart felt heavy every time I passed her by.

She was no longer following me everywhere at my heels. She was burying herself in a blanket on her dog bed. She had trouble going to the restroom, and all of her lively traits were watered down. I took one picture of her two days before my birthday. She hadn't come out of her bed. Within that week, the lump grew to be double in size. I had never seen anything grow so quickly. Two days after my birthday, I took her to the emergency vet hospital with my ex-mother-in-law. The lump began to bleed and leak.

When the veterinarian came in, it was like I was experiencing dejavu. The same end of life talk. The same details about what kind of quality of life she would have, or if she would be suffering more-trying to escape the inevitable. After complimenting me on how well Princess was taken care of, she gave me a moment to decide. The same as Peewee, she looked me in the eyes, and I knew that her time had come. She was letting me know that she was at the end of her line, and I couldn't do her a disservice by trying to prolong her suffering just because I wasn't ready for her to go. Within days, I went from having my furry child in my lap, to picking up her urn days later. She and Peewee now sit on my dresser until I find a forever place to put them.

In the timeframe after I went through my extremely un-healthy downward spiral, many people asked me when I would "get back out there." When would I start looking for my special someone again? My answer was always the same in which I would tell them that I wasn't looking for anyone, or I just didn't need anyone. I didn't have a good feeling about the idea of putting myself out there anymore. What if they thought I was damaged goods? What if they rejected me, as I had been in the past? No, I'm good.

I was at work, and it was pretty routine. I hadn't been working there extremely wrong at this point, and it wasn't long until I had made friends with most of the guys that I worked with. There were just a couple of my co-workers that kept to themselves, and I understood that. We're there to make money, not try to make best friends with someone, or at least that's not the intent.

There was one guy that I worked with, and after I passed by his work area and made small talk, he became one out of a few people that I would've been okay talking to everyday. We would go to lunch, and after time, I noticed that this was one of the kindest, non-judgmental people I had ever met. After some time, we became closer, and long story short, we decided to take a crack at dating. I'm so glad that I did, because this man changed my world for the better.

Was it a little stressful keeping a relationship at work? Sure. Had we been having this discussion before I began a relationship with this man, I would've advised against it. Part of me still would, because I've witnessed other work relationships, and they crashed and burned with horrendous outcomes. I made sure the correct people knew when I started my relationship, and disclosed what I needed to. There are companies, of course, that either frown upon this, or completely forbid it. I received the chance to do right, and keep my relationship out of the workplace, and I would say we were successful, because everyone else didn't find out until years later when we got married.

This is the first relationship in my adult life that I felt I was a part of a team. I have grown so much since being with my husband, and I wouldn't trade it for the world. I know that this man is on my team, and while it hasn't been easy, I know that the best things don't come easy. I have confided in my husband my most terrible secrets, and have expected him to turn his back on me, but he didn't. We're not perfect, but I believe our imperfections make us at least the perfect fit for each other. Corny, right? Yeah, I know. Sorry.

The point is this: I'm not a psychic, and I'm not a life coach. I can't sit here and predict that if you go through enough shit in your life, that things will look up soon after. I wish I could say that, or tell you the equation for a happy life, because everyone is different. Your situation could either run parallel to mine, or we could have not one thing in common. All I can do is be completely honest with you about my life, and my indiscretions, and let you do with this information as you will.

I believe that all in all, it wasn't just the support of a few that got me through my tough times. It was also finding myself a purpose. If it weren't being a mother to my daughter, it would've been my career choices. I have made the major decisions in my life, because I wanted to be able to stand on my own. As you have read, I didn't have the full support of those I should be able to consider family. With that, I don't write these things out as a hit-list. I'm not here to bash anyone, but I am here to explain some reasons as to why I'm not as emotionally inept as others should be by this point in their lives.

My story doesn't necessarily have a happy ending. While I've ironed out some details in how I want to run my life, I still deal with the chaos inside myself that prevents me from being completely happy. Due to my lack of healthy relationship examples, I have been slowly navigating my way through my current marriage. I have had reasons in the past not to trust whoever I was with, and if I let my demons get the better of me, I would keep going through the vicious cycle that is ugly insecurity.

In my eyes, my husband can do no wrong. Again, are we perfect? Of course not, but day in, and day out, we try. We falter, and after many trials and errors, we come back stronger. We apologize, and we recognize our own faults. I have questioned his loyalty more times than I care to admit, and that wasn't because he was doing wrong, but in my mind I couldn't fathom having a partner that was worth a damn—that was worth my trust. He chose me constantly, every single time, and he has loved me even when I didn't deserve it.

Chapter 27

It wasn't until this past year that some of the issues I was harboring began to calm down. While they weren't, and aren't, cured. I consistently go to therapy, and have been on a constant stream of medications to treat my depression, and anxiety. As if things hadn't been strange enough, I began to experience strange, new symptoms. I got a referral to a new psychiatrist, and from day one he got me. It was like I knew him for years. I had my initial conversation with him, and he asked me one question no one ever had.

"Has anyone ever asked you if you're bi-polar?" He asked.

I was surprised. I never had that asked of me outside of dry humor. I told him that it wasn't a conversation that I ever had, and after more time talking, he prescribed a medication used to treat bi-polar disorder. All of these years I've been treating depression, and anxiety, everyone completely missed that chance that I could be bi-polar. So, my main symptoms were never addressed. I finally felt...whole.

I stayed on that medication, and came off of the other psychiatric medications. I felt good. Months and months passed. I was going to work, and began to feel strange. I went to talk to my main manager as we had a history of being blatantly honest. I sat down, and as I began to talk, he tilted his head to the side. He told me in that conversation that I didn't look well, and he could see it in my eyes that something was wrong. In my mind, I knew that he was right. Something wasn't right.

He told me that everyone cared about me, and it wasn't that I wasn't wanted, but he wanted me to go home, and not come back until my mental health got straightened out. So, that's what I did. I grabbed my stuff, and walked to my car. I didn't realize that my husband was in tow, but when I did, I explained the conversation that I had, and what my immediate plan was. I spent a month and a half being confined to my home.

Not being able to sleep was my first symptom. Every night I wouldn't go to sleep until about 11 P.M., and like clockwork, I would wake up at 3 A.M. The thing was that I wasn't tired. I would wake up, and I would move all day long without stopping. I felt like I was on speed. I cleaned my home, I organized literally everything. I had racing thoughts like no other time, just trying to figure out what the next task was.

If you're not familiar with bi-polar disorder, the best way I can describe it would be a fluctuation of moods between depression, and super highs. If the highs get to a certain level, you experience mania. Less severe highs are called hypomania. I was experiencing mania, with an uncomfortable feeling of elation, and hyperactivity. I couldn't bring myself down. If I weren't busy doing something, I would constantly pace back, and forth. I would often check the floors for wear marks.

My body would be exhausted, but my mind wasn't having it. Sleep was extremely difficult as I was beginning to hear noises. Medically speaking, I don't think extremely sensitive hearing is a symptom, but it was for me. My family coined me, "Bat Ears," because I swear I could hear just about anything. Sounds cool? In a sense, I guess. I had such sensitive hearing that I couldn't listen to anything at the normal volume I usually would. Any elevated sound made me feel like my ear drums were going to burst. Conversations were at a whisper, even the ticking of the turn signal in my car made me want to cry.

I spoke to my psychiatrist, and I was prescribed medications that would typically work on those with bi-polar. Guess what? Not me. I tried two different medications before we got to the third one, and I felt relief within the first week. The first two escalated my symptoms, and I was miserable. The amount of abnormal noise I was hearing was making me feel like I was completely losing it. That third medication—which I'm still on—is my saving grace. I must've slept for what felt like forever when I finally came down from the mania.

This condition is manageable. I'm a little upset that it took me all these years to find the one psychiatrist that knew how to help me, but I'm here, and I'm grateful. I was fortunate enough to have a workplace that recognized when I wasn't well, or being my better self. I'm sorry to say that many are still many that carry a stigma concerning mental health. That's crap. There is no shame in wanting to be mentally sound, and there's nothing wrong with admitting that you need help. I think people that have the gall to admit that they could improve as a person deserves a lot of respect. We are an imperfect race of human beings that have the capability of being better, yet there are those that still think that it's either a myth, a joke, or both. That's extremely unfortunate.

I told you that I was an empath. Let me tell you the topics that I am extremely passionate about: Mental health, and suicide. Oh, that dirty word. That bad word. That forbidden word. *Suicide.* I won't talk your ear off about it, but I will say that you've read the outline that is my shitshow of a life. Other people have had it a million times worse than myself. It's a shame that when someone takes their life, those left behind will say, "They were always so happy," "They didn't show any signs," "I would've never expected them to take their own life." We have molded ourselves into a society where people either get shamed for their feelings, or ignored.

I'm not going to throw statistics at you, because chances are that you've heard it somewhere before. As an empath, I know myself well enough to know that I become a sponge, and soak up other emotions. I'm sure it drives my husband insane at times, but I feel for those that are facing difficulties with mental health. When I hear people say that they are, or have considered suicide in the past, I cry. I cried like a child, because I was there. Thinking that at multiple times in my life I wasn't good enough to even be alive, or that life was too hard for just me to handle.

I know that mental health doesn't gain enough traction unless it takes someone such as a celebrity. Of course, it's sad. It's said that the happiest people are often the ones dealing with the most. I don't know the science of mental health, and I'm not a doctor. I wish I were, but all I know is the experiences I've had. So, don't take any of this and write it in stone. I'm just a nobody from Texas who watches too much Dr. Phil.

I think this is the end of the road from me to you. I don't have very much else to share. I'm still a work in progress as a mother, a wife, an unprofessional writer, and most importantly, as a human being. Surround yourself with people that bring you up, not drag you down. Society doesn't get to dictate who you allow to be in your life, because you're the one that has to live it—not everyone else. For the ones you do allow, check on them often. I'm not sure if anything I've written will speak to you on any type of level, and I'm really not sure if it can translate into any type of advice, but if you are reading this, and you're imperfectly perfect, I think that you're doing amazingly.

So, with everything else already being said, don't take shit from anyone, be a good person, and love yourself enough to make the tough decisions that only you can make. May your future be in your fortune.

Ang.